Ghost T
of Glouces~~ter's Past~~

THE AUTHOR — Eileen Fry was born in Surrey. Her interest in the history of Gloucester began almost immediately after she came to live in the city with her husband and family in 1974. A trip to the Folk Museum and the Cathedral kindled an interest in local history which became almost a passion.

In 1988 her husband Michael researched a ghost story which led to a discussion with Rosemary Harvey on the local folk ghost stories of Gloucester. Were there any more stories? If so did they fit into the rich historical background of the city? Eileen and Rosemary set off walking around the streets of Gloucester examining the buildings and asking local people what they knew. During the Gloucester summer festival season Eileen and Rosemary entertain visitors and local citizens with their 'Step back in Time ghostly tours'. They also give talks on the subject.

Eileen is a member of the Gloucester Civic Trust and has written this book hoping to preserve the local legends and act as an introduction to the historic background of Gloucester.

Eileen also enjoys writing poems, some of which have been recently published.

Ghost Trails
of Gloucester's Past

A new collection of spine-tingling ghost stories

EILEEN FRY

THE WINDRUSH PRESS · GLOUCESTERSHIRE

First published in Great Britain by
The Windrush Press
Little Window
High Street, Moreton-in-Marsh
Gloucestershire GL56 0LL
1995

Telephone: 01608 652025
Fax: 01608 652125

A catalogue record for this book is available in the British Library

ISBN 0 900075 44 9

Typeset by Archetype, Stow-on-the-Wold

Printed and bound in Great Britain by Biddles Ltd, Guildford

CONTENTS

THE TWENTIETH CENTURY

GLOUCESTER CONNECTIONS

SHADOWS OF THE PAST

AUTHOR'S INTRODUCTION AND ACKNOWLEDGEMENTS

Why a book about ghost stories you may ask? I can only say that some of the wonderful historical stories and legends connected with Gloucester, including the ghost stories often passed down in families deserve a mention before they disappear into oblivion. The City of Gloucester has a rich background of exciting stories some of which are known to us, and others which will never be revealed.

This book is not to convince you that ghosts are a fact. Most people say, 'I will not believe in them until I see one for myself'. This seems to be a very healthy attitude. Most of the people who have made claims to some sort of ghostly encounter say that the experience comforted them and made them more confident in the belief of life after death. If this is so it would seem that each of us has a spiritual life.

Meanwhile we do hope you enjoy reading these stories and appreciate the wealth of history connected to Gloucester.

The first story reminds us of the time when the Romans came here and built a fine town. They had skilled craftsmen and used the very best tools and materials. They named Glevum as a place built to honour Rome. A town to stand forever not just a temporary garrison town. Glevum means a place of light and even now we feel that light is still with us.

Acknowledgements

This book is a collection of some of the many stories I have heard and read about in our Gloucester.

I have had so much support it is very hard to be specific,

but I feel I must mention some of the people who have helped to get this book on the road. My husband Michael has been very tolerant and supportive. Rosemary Harvey has been my investigative partner, and since she touched the blarney stone in Ireland whilst on holiday has become an even better raconteur. Philip Cook, Lesley Pritchard, Naomi and other staff in the Tourism Office have always been helpful. My history tutor, Russell Howes, has astounded me with his local knowledge as has David Browne of *The Citizen* newspaper. The ladies in the Gloucester collection room at the local library, who have always been ready with their expertise. The Civic Trust, Philip Moss, and most important of all the wonderful local people of this city. I have met such a lot of interesting and friendly people in Gloucester and without them this book would not be possible.

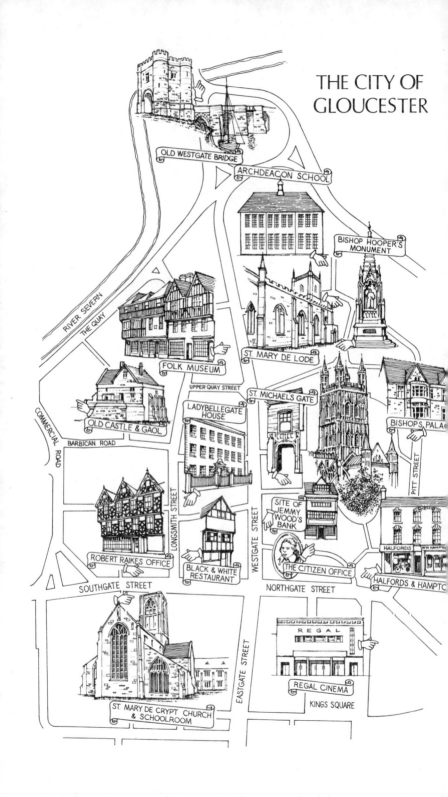

THE CITY OF GLOUCESTER

OLD WESTGATE BRIDGE

ARCHDEACON SCHOOL

BISHOP HOOPER'S MONUMENT

RIVER SEVERN

THE QUAY

FOLK MUSEUM

ST. MARY DE LODE

UPPER QUAY STREET

ST MICHAELS GATE

LADYBELLEGATE HOUSE

BISHOPS PALA

OLD CASTLE & GAOL

COMMERCIAL ROAD

BARBICAN ROAD

PITT STREET

LONGSMITH STREET

SITE OF JEMMY WOOD'S BANK

WESTGATE STREET

HALFORDS   WH HAMPT

ROBERT RAIKES OFFICE

BLACK & WHITE RESTAURANT

THE CITIZEN OFFICE

HALFORDS & HAMPTO

SOUTHGATE STREET

NORTHGATE STREET

EASTGATE STREET

REGAL

ST. MARY DE CRYPT CHURCH & SCHOOLROOM

REGAL CINEMA

KINGS SQUARE

ROMAN GLOUCESTER

The Handsome Ghosts of Glevum

In fifty years after the birth of Jesus Christ the Romans decided to build a new town which they would call Glevum, place of light.

They called in all their best planners to set about and build a place to the honour of Rome. They were a clever and sophisticated bunch, and labour was no problem. Trained to be fit and strong the men of the Roman army used all the skills and brawn necessary to build the place we now live in and know as Gloucester.

What a task they set themselves. The fine roads they constructed all across the country became the basis of our transport system today. Little did they know that one day juggernauts, lorries and other heavy traffic would be rushing along the routes. They had in mind chariots and carts drawn by horses when they made their plans.

Once their fortress was complete in about 65 AD, they later undertook to build a fine strong wall around the city. This would protect the Romans from marauding bands of barbarians who roamed around the land. Wolves too would be howling at night looking for a meal.

The soldiers given the task of the night watch must have talked about friends they had left behind them. The young soldiers, often only sixteen years of age, would walk the wall in pairs with their cloaks wrapped close around them, shields and heavy spears at the ready. How relieved they must have been when dawn arrived and they could sleep.

Soldiers from all parts of the Roman empire signed on for a service of twenty years with no choice of where they would be posted. This meant that many would never return to their own country. What a bleak cold prospect that must have been. The warmth of Rome would compare sadly to the cold winds of Glevum chilling them to the bone. Just by Gloucester Cross they built fine baths where they could meet their friends and relax after a hard day's work. They would talk about the new Roman empire and how it was growing.

Some of the soldiers by coming here escaped persecution. Christians were thrown to the lions for sport, so even our cold shores must have been preferable. The Christians met in secret and their sign of brotherhood was a fish. A wreath of laurels represented a promised triumph. It is believed the first Christians to worship in Gloucester met in the house of a high ranking officer built just outside the Roman wall. Where now stands the Church of St Mary de Lode a tessellated floor was discovered which is now four feet below the foundations. The secret sign of the fish was worked into the mosaic stone floor.

High ranking officers were sometimes allowed to bring their families with them. Fine houses were built just outside the walled city. I wonder if any of our citizens have Roman blood in their veins?

When a Roman died the body would be taken outside of the wall and buried often quite close to the road. The Kingsholm district of Gloucester was one of several sites used for this purpose. Over the years many Roman discoveries have been made, and the City Museum in Brunswick Road has splendid examples of Roman treasures found in the burial places.

If ghosts are to be found in Gloucester can it be surprising that we were told of a story in the Denmark Road area which was once on the route to the first fortress at Kingsholm?

A lady told me that one evening when climbing the stairs of her house she was amazed to see two ghostly Roman soldiers apparently walking on air. The men were very plain to see and she can still remember them well. One man was dressed in a mauve cloak, and the other in a dark blue loose fitting garment. The men were engaged in deep conversation and did not notice her as she passed by them. Our lady said she felt no fear and even went so far as to say 'Good Morning,' to them. There was no response and she felt they were not aware of her standing there in the present age. Two nights after, the lady saw the same two soldiers again walking along. This time she did not approach but watched with interest.

A third time the same apparition appeared, and the lady said she felt sure they were officers of a high rank as they looked so well dressed and important. The woman then felt the time had come to call in her priest in order to put their souls at rest. The man of God called and prayers were said. The men were not seen again.

When discussing her experience the lady said she later regretted calling in the priest as the soldiers were so good looking.

MEDIEVAL AND TUDOR GLOUCESTER

++
The Death of Edward II and Gloucester
• •

The death of Edward II in Berkeley Castle led to great prosperity for the abbey: a terrible and cruel murder which took place at the castle in the year 1327 on 21 September had a lasting effect on Gloucester and its prosperity.

At that time Abbot Thokey a capable and visionary architect was head of St Peters in Gloucester. He saved the aisle from collapse when he built buttresses to strengthen the outside walls. This was a long and lengthy process, so when Edward II in happier times visited the abbey, the abbot proudly showed him the new building, and entertained Edward as his guest.

It is said that Edward whilst dining remarked on the portraits of former kings hanging in the hall. He asked if his own likeness would one day be amongst them. The abbot is said to have made the prophetic reply, 'I hope to have your majesty in a more honourable position than any of these'. The words were noted and repeated many a time after that occasion. Edward as a young man was gifted, intelligent and handsome. He was educated mainly by monks and was fond of art, drama and gardening. He had no disposition to be a king, but as the only son in a household of sisters was obliged to take the throne. Edward was an equally reluctant bridegroom when a marriage was arranged with the attractive teenager Isabella of Boulogne. It was hoped that marriage would change his homosexual tendencies. The French connection was also essential for

4

diplomatic reasons. Piers Gaveston however remained Edward's favourite companion, and unwisely the king made no attempt at discretion.

Isabella was pregnant with the first of her four children when, during a bloody battle at Blacklow Hill, whilst attempting to repel the warring Scots a tragedy occurred. Edward's cousin, Thomas Earl of Lancaster, resenting the interference and influence of Piers seized the chance to plot with other noblemen. The angry men goaded by jealousy held Piers and he was beheaded.

Edward was devastated, but this did not change him for later it was said that the son of Hugh Despenser replaced Piers as his favourite. Queen Isabella now the mother of four children hated the Despenser and was delighted when an opportunity to return to France presented itself. Isabella took a lover. His name was Roger Mortimer and they openly lived together in France. They plotted together and re-turned to England hoping to take over from the luckless king. Isabella made a dramatic arrival supported by a Dutch army. Roger was by her side. Edward hearing about the approaching confrontation left London and spent two days with Abbot Thokey in Gloucester. He then fled to Cardiff.

Hugh Despenser and his son, the friends of the king, were sought out and killed in the most horrible manner possible at that time. They were dragged along by a horse, then hanged, drawn and quartered. A gory and bloody end to the royal favourites. Isabella and Roger were welcomed in London and the king was obliged to abdicate the throne in favour of his young son. Edward III was crowned in Westminster. The queen now believed she had the power of England's rule in her hands.

Edward was now imprisoned in Kenilworth Castle, but he was not entirely forgotten. An unsuccessful plot was made to free him and the queen became anxious. It was decided to remove the deposed Edward to a more secure place of residence. Berkeley Castle seemed an ideal choice as it was much more out of the way than Kenilworth and its walls were high and forbidding. Eagerly the queen promised money to help with the extra soldiers needed.

Edward was moved with ceremony from Kenilworth to Berkeley Castle. Thomas of Berkeley was personal escort on this journey anxious to see there was no trouble on the way. Edward requested that he could again visit the Abbot Thokey in Gloucester. It was Easter time and on Palm Sunday the sad procession made its way into Gloucester. This was the last time Edward would visit the city alive.

Murder in Berkeley Castle

Thomas of Berkeley undertook the responsibility of Edward's imprisonment in the castle. He was pleased to do this because he felt in some way he could exact vengeance for the way his estates and property had suffered when the Despensers plundered his land. He also received a large amount of money to pay for soldiers and food. He was happy to watch over Edward and assured the queen of his constant personal attention. After an abortive rescue attempt led by a Stephen Dunhead, Edward was placed in solitary confinement. It seemed that even though he was in prison there were still people eager for his release. Roger and Isabella knew that every day his presence was a threat to them. They wanted a permanent answer to the problem. A terrible plot was hatched. On the 21 September 1327, five hired assassins rushed into the room where Edward lay resting. Although weakened by imprisonment he was still a strong man and must have fought hard for his life. He was outnumbered and his desperate cries were heard all over the castle. It is said that a red hot poker and a horn were used to carry out the dreadful murder. This made sure that there were no visible injuries on the body of Edward. This method had been used to kill homosexuals before.

Servants who had heard the cries of the king were unable to remain silent. The story went around the little village of Berkeley then was passed by travellers to Gloucester. In no time at all the manner of Edward's death was no longer a secret. Tongues were wagging everywhere.

The King's Last Resting Place

Things were going wrong for Isabella. She had hoped that the death of the deposed king would cause little fuss and soon be forgotten, but she miscalculated the loyalty of the people. Hearing of the manner of the death, rumours instead of diminishing grew louder. Something had to be done to appease the masses. The body of the king was kept in state at the castle. Nobles came to honour the remains. Awkward questions were asked, people wanted to know when his burial would take place. Important clergy were approached but fearing involvement in the sordid mess, excuses were made. No one wanted to risk upsetting Isabella. It seemed more prudent to refuse.

Abbot Thokey Agrees to Accept the Body of Edward II

Eventually Abbot Thokey was approached. He had, after all, known Edward in happier times and had been his religious adviser and remembering how Edward had admired the structure of his abbey in Gloucester, he found it impossible to deny his soul the honour of burial.

What Did They See?

One Saturday night a group of lads were making their way home after a night of revelry at the local pub. They were a lively lot jesting and jostling their happy way home. It was the weekend and work was out of mind. The tall wall of Berkeley Castle loomed up as they crossed the road. This did not impress them as they were more than accustomed to the castle as three of them actually lived in the village and the other two just a short distance away.

Bob was the first to stop in his tracks. He was transfixed to the spot and the others too. It was a dark night but not too dark to see the strange and amazing sight in front of them. A large door in the side of the wall was open and a sombre sight met their eyes. Soldiers on horseback followed by soldiers on foot walked along, and set off down the road. Not ordinary soldiers as they knew them, but men seemingly dressed in old fashioned attire, their heads bowed, were moving along. They were escorting a large horse dray, with large wooden wheels and monks with dark cowled hoods walked behind. One monk appeared to be moving his way to lead the procession. They did not notice the night revellers standing there or anything else.

Some believed the men, others ridiculed them saying it was the effects of a Saturday night out, but even to this day Bob still stands by what he said eighteen years ago. His niece sometimes asks him to repeat the story. It is always the same. Why did the ghostly procession appear that night? Why were they the ones to see it? Sometimes they wish they had waited to see the event in more detail. Other times they wish they had not seen it at all, for all the stick they get. They remain convinced it was the dray carrying the body of Edward II at the beginning of its journey to Gloucester.

At night sometimes, other Berkeley folk have claimed to hear shouting and cries ringing through the night. Perhaps that too has a connection with events which took place in 1327.

Edward II's Last Visit to Gloucester

As the solemn funeral procession made its way from Berkeley Castle to Llanthony Priory on the way to Gloucester it is said local villagers left the fields and other work to watch the impressive cortège. Large black horses pulled the cart and monks chanted as they went along. Hushed voices began to question the terrible way the king had died.

A procession of the whole city it is claimed eventually led the body of the king into the abbey. Eventually he was buried near the high altar. Pilgrims flocked to see the tomb.

Eager to impress the visitors with his own piety the young King Edward III erected a lavish and elaborate alabaster monument over the tomb of his dead father. A splendid gothic canopy covered the royal effigy, and

Edward II's monument in Gloucester Cathedral

remains in the cathedral to this day. It has been described as 'one of the glories of mediaeval sculpture and decorative tabernacle work'. It is suggested that the effigy was copied from a wax mask taken after death.

Was the Ghostly Coffin in the Cathedral?

A dear lady who loves Gloucester Cathedral greatly and is a regular worshipper there, told me a very strange story in confidence one day. It seems that after taking communion the lady, still feeling emotional after receiving the sacrament, made her way down the steps towards the rear of the cathedral. She saw in the corner where the book stall and gift shop now stands a vision of brightness. There were hundreds of candles lit and shining where they had been placed around an impressive coffin draped with material. Drawn to the sight the lady made her way to the light. Her friend softly took her arm and said she was going in the wrong direction. The moment was gone and realising the coffin was no longer there she changed her route.

When at a later time she sat down and collected her thoughts, the lady pondered on what she had seen and now says that she feels sure that she had experienced a time slip, and the vision was no other than the coffin of Edward II lying in state and waiting for burial.

A Prosperous City

Word soon spread that the tomb of Edward II was a real sight to see. The people were now satisfied that sufficient respect had been given to the relics of their deceased king. If he had suffered in death, at least his resting place gave him honour.

St Peters Abbey became a great place for pilgrims. Visitors came from all over England and even from Europe. Pilgrims can be likened to the tourists of today. Groups of people would set off in order to pay respects to martyrs, and if they enjoyed themselves on the way, stopping at hostelries, swapping yarns and having a jolly time, well it was so much the better. They would pray for dead souls

New Inn Yard

and hope to increase their spirituality which would count in the life to come. Those unable to spare the time to visit personally would pay professional pilgrims to holiday at their expense. They were then expected to pray for the sponsor on the way. The pilgrims would often wear a large tall black hat, on which to pin the badges of the places they had visited and carry a stout staff to help them on the way.

No visitor would arrive without payment. Many would give large amounts to prove their piety. Noblemen and princes soon joined the queue, as the abbey became more and more popular. The abbot was delighted, now the order was able to enlarge the buildings and spend great amounts on making the abbey even more attractive. The wonderful cloisters with their fan vaulted ceilings were built with the money from pilgrims. Some of the pilgrims returned home with stories of miracles experienced in Gloucester. This made others keen to see for themselves. What had been a kind gesture on the part of Abbot Thokey to accept Edward's body for burial, now become a blessing. How vexed the monks at Malmesbury, Winchester and Bristol must have been to think they had turned down such a lucrative opportunity.

The green in the cloisters was used for revelling, but the monks soon realised this was most inconvenient. As there was no problem with finance they built inns for the comfort and accommodation of visitors. Under the supervision of a monk, John Twyning, an old hostelry was pulled down and a fine New Inn erected in its place. This was then claimed to be the largest hostelry in the country.

The Fleece Inn was another place built for the guests. In no time at all Gloucester was known for its hospitality and entertainment.

King Henry II and Rosamunde in Gloucestershire

The European Union causes many heated discussions and one of the topics most likely to be argued is our reliance on the good will of the French. Why should the French people have an influence on our policies we ask, let them remain on their own side of the channel.

The history books will tell us that for many years we have been under the rule of the French. We have benefitted from the fine buildings they constructed in our country, and liaisons of a romantic nature were common. One such an example was in Gloucester when King Henry II ruled in 1154–1189.

Henry was a Frenchman born in 1133. He could speak very little English and originally spent most of his time in France. This did not prevent him from keeping a firm rule on our country, and he tried to control our politics. Whenever he thought it necessary he would leave France and come to England. He liked to keep his finger on the pulse.

The king was always a well known visitor to Gloucestershire. When Flaxley Abbey was granted a charter, a grand ceremony was attended by the young Henry. At the celebrations Henry noticed a young woman named Rosamunde Clifford. She was a local maiden from Frampton on Severn and you can see Rosamunde's Green at Frampton today. Rosamunde's fair complexion and flaxen hair made her appear different from the young girls in his own country, and she no doubt found the dark eyes and the French accent of Henry equally appealing. It is said she was eighteen at the time and he was twenty. The two met and became lovers. In a short while Rosamunde bore him two sons. The ill-fated couple knew from the beginning that marriage was unacceptable, and Henry was forced to return to France when he became king.

Back in France Henry realized he must make a proper royal marriage and again fell in love, this time with Eleanor. At first their union was said to be a happy one and Eleanor had nine children. Unfortunately as a queen, Eleanor became very interested in politics and would often quarrel with the decisions made by her husband. Eleanor also became suspicious of the frequent visits her husband made to Gloucester. It is said that her discovery of a silk embroidery thread on one of Henry's spurs made her wonder if his reasons were entirely political.

Eleanor and Henry were in constant verbal conflict. She encouraged the sons of the marriage to fight in battle against Henry. All but Henry's favourite son John turned against him, and even he was against his father at the end. Henry II felt he could not tolerate the situation with Eleanor any longer. She was sent off to Salisbury in England and remained there under house arrest for sixteen years.

Henry II now felt able to continue his relationship with Rosamunde. Once more a scandal was caused, as they enjoyed each other's company. This did not last too long and Rosamunde's death was a sad blow to Henry. She was buried at Godstone Priory in Woodstock.

Flaxley Abbey

When the charter was granted to Flaxley Abbey by Henry II the area was at that time within the boundaries of the

Flaxley Church and Abbey

Forest of Dean. The Cistercian Monks were known as the white monks because of their warm white cassocks. Part of the charter read: 'Know ye that I have granted and confirmed to God and St Mary and to the monks of the Cistercian order, a certain place in the valley called Flaxley to build an abbey there. Half of my wood at Dymock, and half my nets which I have in my hands, for the convenience of my men, because I would have my monks enjoy that part of the wood peaceably and quietly, without any interfering from any other persons'. A grant of two oaks out of the forest every seven days for supplying their iron forge for fuel was provided and a certain protection was required for the grazing of the king's deer and wild beast.

Miracles at St Anthony's Well

At the head of one of the brooks feeding a stream which runs down the Flaxley valley still lies St Anthony's Well. This is a place reputedly used by the monks for bathing until the suppression of the abbey in 1541. St Anthony's Well was a secluded glade overshadowed by a large beech tree and a mossy bank. Local people have for years talked of the healing powers of the water in this well dedicated to St Anthony.

All manner of skin complaints were said to benefit from the qualities of the water. At the beginning of the nineteenth century a stone area was built to enable bathers to slip into the beneficial waters. The clear water is of a very high quality and contains iron and lime. The temperature is said to be 50°F.

Local people still remember the summer days when they would walk to St Anthony's Well and take a sup from the cup provided. Take a thought for St Anthony, King Henry and fair Rosamunde too if you ever visit this enchanting spot.

++

King John and Gloucester

♦ ♦ ♦ ♦ ♦ ♦ ♦ ♦ ♦ ♦ ♦ ♦ ♦ ♦ ♦ ♦ ♦ ♦ ♦ ♦ ♦ ♦ ♦ ♦ ♦ ♦ ♦ ♦

King John also known as John Lackland came to the throne in 1199. He was the youngest son of Henry II and he too was attracted to an English lady from Gloucester. John married Isabella, the daughter of the Sheriff of Gloucester. With the marriage came a great deal of property and acres. No longer would he be scoffed at and named Lackland.

John did not stay too long with Isabella from Gloucester and there were no children from this marriage. They were divorced on the grounds of 'consangunity' being of the same blood. She was his cousin two or three times removed. He replaced our local lady with a French woman again named Isabella. The marriage was extremely stormy even though this time the couple had four children.

St Anthony's Well

John was a scheming king who caused the English to lose most of their possessions in France. The barons rose against John and forced him to set the seal on the Magna Carta which became a cornerstone of English liberty.

Meanwhile back in Gloucester John's wife Isabella was imprisoned within the walls of Gloucester Castle in 1214 after the king allegedly hanged her gallants above her bed.

On the 18 October 1216 when only 49 years of age John died unexpectedly at Newark Castle, Lincolnshire 'after a surfeit of peaches and new cider'. Isabella was released and her first thought was for her young son Henry who had been named after his grandfather.

Henry III: The Boy King Crowned in Gloucester

No book about Gloucester would be complete without the important event which took place in Gloucester Abbey on 27 October 1216. The young boys of King's School in

Gloucester still have a golden circle around their navy caps in rememberence of the crowning of Henry III.

King John had died unexpectedly. He was not at all popular with his barons at the time so upon hearing the news they offered the crown of England to Louis of France.

Whilst others dithered, William the Earl of Pembroke, took it upon himself to make decisions. He commandeered the royal army and vowed to see young Prince Henry take his rightful place upon the throne. William did not trust the barons or Louis of France. Queen Isabella was equally determined to see her son crowned and welcomed the earl to Kingsholm, delighted to be reunited with her son Henry again. Isabella rejoiced that she was now free from the tyranny of her husband John who had given the Abbot of St Peters control over her imprisonment.

A ceremony was arranged and proclaimed to the people. Henry III was crowned King of England in the Abbey of Gloucester which was only a hundred years old. The official crown jewels had been lost in the Wash by King John but Isabella delightedly gave her own circlet to use for the service. The word soon spread around the city, and everyone who was able rushed into the streets with branches of trees and garlands of flowers to greet the first and only king to be crowned in Gloucester. The Bishop of Winchester officiated, as time was vital and it was thought imprudent to wait for the Archbishop of Canterbury who should have performed the ceremony. The small but solemn ten-year-old boy promised on the relics of the saints to keep the laws of England. He also promised to keep up the payment of 1,000 marks to be paid annually to Rome.

The Earl of Pembroke presented the prince saying: 'Although we have persecuted the father of this young prince for his evil demeanour, yet this child is pure and innocent of his father's doings. We must therefore of duty and conscience pardon this young and tender prince. He must be our sovereign King and Governor, let us remove from us this Louis, the French King's son and suppress his

Llanthony Priory

people who are a confusion and shame to our nation. Let us cast off the yolk of servitude from our shoulders.'

Henry III never forgot the welcome given to him in Gloucester and always regarded the city as his real home. He preferred it to London and spent as much time as he could in Gloucester. He was a conscientious and religious king who always tried to do his best for his subjects. Henry passed a charter giving Gloucester the right to hold a guild and other markets. The abbey was given the tithe of all the boars killed in the Forest of Dean. The forest became known as The King's Forest at Gloucester. There were at the time more boars in the forest then anywhere else in the country, so wild boar was definitely on the menu for the monks of Gloucester.

King Henry later married a French lady from Provence named Eleanor. They worked closely together sharing a love of beautiful buildings and they were a pious couple. In Gloucester Henry gave money to the Priory Hospital of St Bartholemew now known as the Westgate Galleria, and Whitefriars Priory, a Dominican order. There was at that time also a convent of Whitefriars and a convent of Grey

Friars which made six religious orders in the small City of Gloucester including St Oswalds Priory. Llanthony Priory also stood just outside the boundaries. There was a saying which was known throughout the country, 'As sure as God's in Gloucester.' It was said that one could walk only fifty yards before passing either a monk or friar.

The Forest of Dean provided the wood for most of the city buildings. Fires were a real hazard. In 1223 a fierce fire broke out at the Cross. The shops belonging to the drapers and shoemakers in that area were destroyed before the long poles used for pulling down blazing buildings could be put to use.

King Henry, whilst planning and taking a personal interest in architecture, struck up a firm friendship with a man called John. He was a mason and was always put in charge of any special building the king had in mind. The two men became firm friends. John was responsible for work in the cathedral, Gloucester Castle and other wonderful buildings in the city. The very best of materials were used, and we can still see the results of his labours. When the great Westminster Abbey was planned King Henry insisted that the only man for the job was John of Gloucester. The mason made the great upheaval of moving to London and Westminster was rebuilt strictly according to the plans of the king. It was said that John of Gloucester was 'King of Masonry in These Realms.'

John was rewarded with land and a property in Gloucester and London. He was exempted from paying taxes. His wages were doubled and he also had a handsome clothing allowance.

Iron from the Forest of Dean was used to help in the construction of Westminster Abbey supplying work for nineteen smiths. After the death of John his son and widow Agnes were granted the revenues of the Manor at Minsterworth. Next time you visit London it may be worth remembering this man from Gloucester was responsible for overseeing Westminster Abbey.

Henry III crowned in Gloucester never forgot his promise to look after the city and the loyal citizens who supported him when he was crowned at only ten years of age.

Henry VIII and Anne Boleyn in Gloucester

No king of England was ever quite so well known or talked about as much as Henry VIII. He was notorious for the way in which he married and then discarded his wives. He caused an uproar in the government of England when he decided to abandon the Catholic Church, and decided that the Pope was no longer head of the Church in England. Monasteries and monks with them had to be demolished, destroyed and all traces of Rome removed. In its place he said the king himself would be defender of the faith and head of the new Church of England. Many say that the real cause of this break which caused murder, death, and destruction was Anne Boleyn. Henry was determined to marry her whatever the consequences.

Divorced, beheaded, died, divorced, beheaded, survived. This is the rhyme many schoolchildren use to remember the fate of the unfortunate six.

The first wife Queen Catherine was a good and loyal wife, who outlived her usefulness. She was an excellent housekeeper and seamstress, who personally made all the king's shirts, and always saw to it that his linen was adequate. In fact one of Anne Boleyn's notorious tantrums was caused by the discovery of a servant secretly taking along linen to the ex-Queen Catherine for her to continue with her task of supplying her former husband with good shirts. Good shirts however were not enough. The king wanted an heir, a son to carry on his line.

Anne Boleyn caught the king's attention and the king cast aside his wife of twenty-two years, Catherine was sent to Ampthill in Bedfordshire to live in the castle there in the 'clean air' and out of the way.

Henry and Anne were married in secret on the 25 January 1533. Courtiers who were quick to spot any tell tale signs questioned the fact that the new queen had cravings for an apple, a fruit she had previously never wanted. Someone was bold enough to suggest that she was with child. Anne burst out laughing, confirming the notion. In fact Anne was three months pregnant at the time of the royal wedding.

On 1 June Anne Boleyn was crowned queen. Her long black hair hung glistening down her back and she carried flowers in her hand. She wore a dress made of crimson brocade and encrusted with precious stones. Around her neck she wore a necklace of pearls larger than peas, and a robe of royal purple was on her shoulders.

After the traditional religious service in Westminster Abbey, not reflecting the break with Rome, the new queen headed a long procession throughout the City of London. It is said that later Anne Boleyn complained to the king that she had seen a great number of caps still on heads and saw but few tongues. People were still considering their opinions on the new queen. They were eager to see her, but that did not mean acceptance.

Princess Elizabeth was born on 7 September 1533. Of course the king had really wanted a boy, but there was still great rejoicing and they hoped next time a boy would be theirs.

In the summer month of July 1535 the king brought Anne with him to visit Gloucester for a four day visit.

The couple were met at Brickhampton bridge near Staverton, as they made their way from Tewkesbury. All the local dignitaries including friars and the clergy were in the procession and the people of Gloucester thronged the streets to see them. Their welcoming speeches were made. Later in Gloucester high mass was sung in the Abbey. After the service the mayor and burgesses presented a petition concerning a sum of £65. The king asked them to wait until he could attend to the matter in London at his leisure.

Anne and the king went hunting around Painswick during their holiday. One night when they returned to the city gates they were delighted to be met by fifteen torch bearers to guide them on the way. This greatly pleased the queen who rewarded them with money.

Eventually on 7 August the royal pair left the city and were escorted to Quedgley Green by the mayor and corporation. It may be that this pleasant break enjoyed by the king was in his mind when later he made the decision to spare the abbey and turn it over to the people to use as a cathedral upon the dissolution of the monasteries. Many abbeys were destroyed upon the king's command but Gloucester was happily an exception. The king would have been reminded that this was the place where a previous Henry had been crowned and Edward II had been buried. He chose to spare the building. Henry VIII also founded the King's School in 1541. King's School Gloucester still remains a very active and popular school in Gloucester. Many readers will have seen the choir and schoolrooms featuring in the TV series *The Choir* written by local author Joanna Trollope.

The holiday in Gloucester may well have been the last happy moments shared by the royal couple for soon after they returned to London things went badly wrong for Anne Boleyn. The king had been attracted to Anne's sharp wit and comments, but now he became irritated with her quick temper and justified criticisms. Two miscarriages met with anger and disappointment. He also had plans concerning the young and comely Jane Seymour of Sudeley Castle in Gloucestershire.

On the 19 May 1536 just nine months after what had been to all intents and purposes a pleasant Gloucester holiday poor Anne Boleyn was executed in the Tower of London. Trumped up charges were made to justify the death. Anne rose and dressed herself carefully on that dreadful morning. It was said that she had never looked so lovely. With peace and dignity she went to her death, saying that 'His Majesty had ever been constant in his career of advancing me from a private woman into a Marchioness then a Queen and now he gives me the innocence of martyrdom'.

After her death Anne's head was removed and placed gently in a piece of cloth. They used an arrow box as a coffin for no proper coffin had been provided. Without ceremony Anne was buried in the little church of St Peter and Vincula, part of the tower complex.

Her mother died just a year later having seen her three children ruined by the king. Her first daughter had been the king's mistress, her son George was executed before Anne, on the false accusation of incest with his sister. Her father died two years later, his world and ambitions in ruin.

There are rumours of a secret burial in the church of St Peter and St Paul in Salle Norfolk. Anne is said to walk there every night on 19 May. Such a terrible execution is bound to be followed by strange rumours. May Anne Boleyn, once Queen of England, rest in peace.

THE EIGHTEENTH CENTURY

Robert Raikes of Gloucester

The Gloucester Journal

How did a wealthy newspaper proprietor of *The Gloucester Journal* become a pioneer in the field of education? What began as a modest attempt to teach poor children to read, snowballed into a tremendous quest to educate every child in the country.

In Southgate Street, on the left is the church of St Mary de Crypt. Just next to this homely church stands what was once a Grammar School of Gloucester founded in the sixteenth century. Many prominent men of the city, whose parents had received their education in this tiny school, not the least of them George Whitefield one of the greatest evangelists of his time. George Whitefield himself when a young man and preparing for the Church dropped some of his earliest writings into the letterbox of Robert Raikes senior. This was the school where Robert Raikes received his lessons also.

If you step inside the church, where Robert Raikes regularly worshipped on a Wednesday and Friday morning, go to the rear and you will find the little side chapel on the south side the chancel now dedicated to children and known as the Robert Raikes Memorial Chapel. Below this is the Raikes family crypt where the great man was buried.

Opposite the church is an attractive black and white building, now a pub which was Robert Raikes house and

The Grammar School

printing works. You can go there for refreshments, if you would like to see where the great man worked. Later he lived in an even grander town house just around the corner which is known as Ladybellgate House. This is now occupied by the legal profession.

Robert Raikes senior was the originator of *The Gloucester Journal* which was first printed on 9 April 1722. At that time provincial newspapers were few and far between, which is further proof that Gloucester was then a place for country gentlemen and people of wealth and learning. The newspaper was very plain by our standards, but it kept the readers in touch with what was going on locally, in London and further afield. Robert Raikes the editor was overjoyed when his first child arrived on 14 September 1735. He was born in the Old Mill House next to the Deanery in Millers Green just behind the cathedral. He was named Robert after his father and grandfather before him. Strangely enough one of his brothers later became a director of the Bank of

England part of which now has its home next to the Docks in Gloucester.

Robert Raikes senior died in 1757 which left the man of our story editor of the thriving newspaper at the early age of twenty-two.

Robert Raikes, the Family Man

Robert was now able to prove that in spite of his youth he could make the newspaper thrive and prosper. He gained quite a reputation in Gloucester for his fashionable clothes. He could be seen strutting around the town with his snuff box on show. He loved good clothes and was by nature a gregarious young man.

As a very eligible gentleman, the ladies around Gloucester were keen to meet Robert Raikes. After a suitable courtship, in 1767 at St James Church in London, Robert married Anne Trigg. She was the only daughter of a well known family from Newnham, her brothers were Sir Thomas Trigg, and Rear Admiral John Trigg. Anne was an excellent wife for Robert. Together they entertained many interesting people. Anne encouraged Robert in his work and supported him. The servants were very loyal to the Raikes family, and were known for their long and faithful service.

The Raikes children consisted of two sons and six daughters plus a further two children who did not survive infancy. The eldest son Robert Napier was born on the very day the first paragraph concerning the Sunday School movement appeared in *The Gloucester Journal*. (3 November 1783.) William Henley Raikes entered the army and became a colonel. Their daughters were Anne, Mary, Albinia, Eleanor, Martha, Charlotte and Caroline. Robert was known as a wise and affectionate father. With such a large family he must have soon realized that discipline of some sort was necessary. There was plenty of opportunity to discover first hand how to cope with ten children, and stay sane at the same time.

♦♦♦

The Highwayman

♦ ♦

This was the time of highwaymen, and a trip by a clothier to Woodchester on his way to Cirencester was described in *The Gloucester Journal* as being interrupted on Crickley Hill by the cry of 'stand and deliver'. The villain was stated as being stout and lusty, five feet eight inches tall, wearing a grey wig, a dark blue coat with gilt buttons, a scarlet waistcoat and a new pair of leather breeches. He was mounted on a large black horse, just the animal for a quick getaway. The highwayman demanded money of the traveller who gave him one guinea and some silver. The highwayman rode off on the Cirencester road. He knew for certain that capture would mean the death penalty.

A lady I spoke to recently told me of one sunny afternoon, whilst on a family picnic on Minchinhampton common she looked up and saw the figure of a highwayman sitting on a large black horse. The experience was a complete surprise, and as she looked down the vision disappeared. She asked her children if they had seen the man too, but she was the only one to notice him. Perhaps it was the ghost of Tom Long the Crickley Hill highwayman, he is still talked about locally and there are crossroads on the common named after him, possibly the spot where he was hanged.

The Amberley Inn at Woodchester is situated in a most beautiful high spot overlooking a valley. It is a very pleasant place in which to spend an evening with a glass of ale or take a meal. The hotel is said by some to still be haunted by Tom Long. I spoke to a local citizen who finds the history of the area so interesting that he has made his own videos on the subject. This gentleman and his wife said that Amberley Inn was said to be the place where Tom Long was taken upon his capture. They spoke of strange footsteps echoing, and doors slamming in the inn. One chef at the inn named Julian was said to grab a Bible when he heard strange noises. Others working there say they have experienced nothing.

My learned photographer friend also said that Culver Hill which passes right by the inn is said to be haunted by a coach on fire driven by a headless driver. There is also the legend of a ghostly nun who walks the common.

Nearby Gatcombe Park has a standing stone opposite the gates with a hole in it. It is claimed that years ago on midsummer's night mothers would pass their babies through the hole and if they were too small, the babies were never seen again. I find this story a bit questionable but who knows? At Woodchester, where the magnificent house there is now open to the public, my friend again said hauntings have been reported. A lady in a long black crinoline dress has been seen. Keys have been heard to rattle in the night and one man claimed to have been thumped in the back.

It is certainly a mystical house well worth a visit.

++
Robert Raikes and Gloucester Prisons
♦ ♦ ♦ ♦ ♦ ♦ ♦ ♦ ♦ ♦   ♦ ♦ ♦ ♦ ♦ ♦ ♦ ♦ ♦ ♦ ♦ ♦ ♦ ♦ ♦ ♦ ♦ ♦ ♦

Highwaymen and other criminals would end up in Gloucester prison and it is here that Robert Raikes saw some of the saddest sights he had ever known. He wrote about the horrors of transportation, 'It will be a dear price to pay for the theft of a couple of geese – not only would the prisoner lose his freedom, but ran the risk of being confined in the hold of a crowded ship, and then be landed in a distant country, probably Australia, where the means of return to England are utterly hopeless.'

Some prisoners in Gloucester jail were described as being half-famished and almost naked. There were no beds, and they slept together in one room. Prisoners were indiscriminated, herded together, regardless of age, sex or offence. Those fortunate enough to have a bit of money were able to buy straw to sleep on. Death was common due to the constant diseases and infections which could thrive in the filthy conditions. Robert Raikes made it his business to visit the prisons and through his columns he

The Old County Gaol

complained of the conditions and asked local people for money to help feed the prisoners.

Mr Raikes tried to give the prisoners hope, and if he found anyone able to read he encouraged them to teach the others. He gave the teachers a small wage out of his pocket. It gave everyone something to do. He wanted desperately to find a useful way to occupy their time. He wanted to give them self-respect. The chairman of the Gloucestershire magistrates Sir George Onesiphorus Paul was an energetic co-worker. A new jail was built in Southgate Street with better conditions for everyone. This has since been pulled down.

Every prisoner was to have a clean separate cell with a window. Indeed the building and the discipline carried out in it, was a model for the gaols in the United States when a commission from that country visited Gloucester.

Robert Raikes and the Children

We now have a good picture of the sort of man we have before us. Robert Raikes was a jolly kindly man who liked to help out his fellow men when he saw the need. He was not afraid to put his hand in his own pocket if he thought it was necessary. It is said that the seeds for his Sunday Schools were sown in the prisons of Gloucester. Prevention being better than cure became his guideline. He must have been broken-hearted when he saw young children of only twelve years of age making their way to the scaffold. This was the age of the death sentence. The crimes prisoners committed were, by today's standards, trivial, and would probably be rewarded by probation in our thankfully more understanding society.

In Search of a Gardener

One fine Sunday morning Robert Raikes set out for a stroll. He was in need of a gardener and upon recommendation had been given the address of a man named Tom who lived in the St Catherine's Meadows area of Gloucester. Robert would have made his way down Westgate Street past the little shops, fine town houses, and the gentlemen's club. Then to the rows of small mean crowded houses where Tom the gardener lived.

Mr Raikes would normally have no cause to travel in this area, indeed it may well have been his first visit. To his horror the streets were full of noisy shouting children. They were fighting, swearing and pushing each other about. He spoke to a woman there who may well have been the wife of Tom the man he was seeking. He asked her where the children lived and why they were fighting. He also passed comment on the state of the wretched rags they were wearing. 'Ah Sir,' the woman replied, 'the children are indeed a terrible example of what it is like in this neighbourhood. All day on a Sunday they are shouting and cursing in the street, playing at chuck and carrying on. It is not really their fault Sir, for all the rest of the week they are working in the pin factory. This is their only free day. There is no room for them in the houses.'

Mr Raikes said it was a shame there was nothing better for them to do. The woman told him that Reverend Stock had tried to teach some of them to read, but that it was an impossible task. Mr Raikes told the woman that the farmers too were full of complaints of the damage to the fields caused by the children on a Sunday. Shaking his head Robert Raikes left Tom's wife to her chores.

Many years later an American named Dr Kennedy from Connecticut told how Mr Raikes had taken him to the spot where all this took place, and described with tears rolling down his face how suddenly he had paused that day and looked up to the sky with a prayer asking if nothing could be done. He said he heard a voice in reply say '"Try." I can never pass that spot without remembering that word that came into my head. I thank God for putting such an idea into my head.'

Setting off to see Thomas Stock who was then the headmaster of King's School as well as the rector of St John's Church in Northgate Street and curate of St Aldates, Robert Raikes was looking for answers.

Action into Reality

Thomas Stock was a vigorous young man who had been to Keble College in Oxford. He was a busy clergyman with many duties and responsibilities but was pleased to take on the job of superintendent of the School on a Sunday venture. He also promised to put forward one third of the expenses.

The two men together worked out a plan to help the poor of the parish. Four women were found who were able to read and willing to exchange their Sunday of peace for a day of toil and perseverance. The ladies were by no means trained for the task and used their own front parlour as a classroom often fitting in as many as fifty children into the tiny room. Mr Raikes paid the women one shilling a day.

Robert Raikes personally went visiting the houses where the pin factory children lived. He asked parents about their children, and they told him they were unable, due to poverty, to give the children clothes suitable to wear to church or a Sunday School. Robert replied that he did not mind what the children wore, all he asked was that their faces and hands were clean and hair combed.

One of the rhymes taught by a Sunday School teacher was

Clean Hands, Clean Face and tidy combed hair,
'Tis better than fine clothes to wear.

To take pride in a clean appearance, was the first step towards self respect, Robert Raikes wisely figured.

This may sound simple to us with our plentiful supply of water, but it was not so easy for parents in those days. A family would be lucky to possess one comb between them. Robert Raikes would often give combs out as a reward for good behaviour.

One of the earliest schools was held in the house of a Mr James King who became the teacher. A Mrs Brabant taught in Oxbody Lane, another in St Aldate's Square, another in Hare Lane and one in Deacon Street, then one of the worst parts in the city. Robert Raikes' own school was held in a house opposite the south porch of St Mary de Crypt Church – the church where he was laid to rest in the crypt (with his family). Mrs Sarah Critchley was the teacher.

Sundays in Gloucester

Sunday mornings in Gloucester soon became the talk of the town. People would turn out to laugh at the sight of the elegant Mr Raikes followed by the ragged pin factory children walking along the road after him. They likened him to the Pied Piper of Hamelin.

The seven o'clock service in the Lady Chapel of Gloucester Cathedral would be attended by Robert Raikes and several of his followers. At the end of the service a jovial Mr Raikes would dip into his pockets and often give the children pennies, sweets or gingerbread. This service was also attended by Mr Jemmy Wood the wealthy banker who unlike Mr Raikes would keep his hands firmly in his pocket.

The Sunday School children were a mixed bunch of children, both in age and abilities. Mrs Critchley in Southgate Street had a very difficult job. A boy named Bill Bates one day brought a badger into her parlour which

Robert Raikes

must have caused chaos. The only books they had were old
Bibles which the teachers had managed to beg and borrow
from anyone interested in the cause. It did not take too long
before criticism turned to reluctant praise. Grateful parents
would stop Mr Raikes in the Gloucester streets and thank
him with tears in their eyes for the change he had made to
the lives of their children. Many were now able to get better
jobs, and improve their position in life. It was also noticed
that they were kinder to each other.

Factory owners were also aware that workers who had
been unruly and hard to manage, now were polite and
reasonable. Beatings were not nearly so necessary. They
even looked more presentable, and some because they

were able to read became even more useful. Sometimes the clever ones were able to help with the reading on the papers which came from customers. Farmers too were happy as the crops were able to flourish without distur-bance. The prisons were no longer full of children. The Gloucester magistrates passed a vote at the quarter sessions in 1786 stating that the merit of the Sunday Schools to the morals of the rising generation was very evident and the community gave thanks to the gentleman promoting them.

The work spread all over the country. When the good results became evident everyone wanted to help: Baptists, Methodists, Quakers all joined in with the movement. Many kindly educated ladies offered to teach children to read and understand the Bible.

At her home in Windsor, Queen Charlotte, the wife of George III, sent for Robert Raikes and wanted to know all about the way he was helping the poor people of the country. She said she envied him his work, and wished there was more she could do. After this visit all the fashionable ladies at Windsor, and indeed everywhere spent their Sundays teaching the poorest of children. Education for everyone was on its way.

The movement spread to the Continent, Austria, Hol-land, Sweden, Norway, Denmark. The American Foreign Sunday School was formed. Then Canada, Australia, Brazil, South America and Japan – all the world was benefitting from the efforts of our man Robert Raikes of Gloucester. We must be proud of him.

Family Tree

Mrs Geraldine Roe of Tunbridge Wells made a trip to Gloucester in October 1994 to discover the home of her ancestor Robert Raikes. The lady revealed her maiden name was Raikes and discovered the Gloucester connection through an old copy of Chambers Encyclopedia which had belonged to her father, Robert Fitzgerald Raikes, late of the Indian Army.

Mrs Roe said she felt as if she was coming home when

she arrived in Gloucester. Geraldine made her own private pilgrimage to the Raikes Chapel at St Mary de Crypt Church. Here she met David Brazington the rector and they compared her own family tree to that of Duncan Raikes. Mrs Roe then went on to the local library and then to the Records Office. She has now decided to donate her family tree which was researched by Joseph Foster and published in 1930 to the Local History Collection.

Mrs Roe is not the last surviving member of this illustrious family. Her daughter Serena Dawn Roe so far has this honour. Mrs Roe is the great-great-great-great-great granddaughter of William Raikes 1737–1808. William was the brother of the famous Robert (born 24 September 1736 and died 5 April 1811).

The Pin Factory Ghost

You may now want to hear more about the lives of the children who were forced to spend their lives working and rising at six o'clock in the morning in order to add to the family income.

Children as young as seven would begin their working lives at the Pin Factory in Westgate Street, one of several in the city. They would go with their older brothers and sisters dragging their cold feet across the cobbled streets, clutching the lumps of bread they would eat for their lunch break. Small hands were nimble and better able to fill the cards with the tiny pins later to be used by dressmakers to make fashionable clothes for fine ladies. The tiny workers would drag their tired bodies up the wooden steps of the old house converted into a factory which had become their place of employment.

This place is now the Folk Museum of Gloucester, which children still like to visit, but for pleasure not for employment. Few visitors fully appreciate the hardships suffered by the pin factory workers. The advantage of the pin factory was the warmth. In the cold wintry days at least the furnace was always burning to help in the manufacture of pins.

Light was needed, so that little eyes were able to see where the pins were going, as they pricked holes into the cards. Sitting cross-legged, hundreds of pins were carded. If the workers became tired or slow they would be scolded with a sharp dig or clout to remind them why they were there. Sometimes they would shout and swear in an attempt to stick up for themselves, fights would break out, but they would be too small or too tired to cause much of a problem. They knew the work was needed to survive. Finally at four in the winter or six in the summer the workers were allowed to return home. Hopefully there would be enough food for the family when they got there. The older children looked after their younger brothers or sisters. The parents did the best they could on their low wages. These were the very children that Robert Raikes took along to Sunday School and then spoke kindly to them. No wonder they were so surprised that anyone had noticed them.

When you go to the Folk Museum, make sure you have a good look around. The place is a real treasure trove of mysteries from long ago. Sometimes to this day a small pin has been found caught up in the floor boards. The people working in the museum know so much about old Gloucester and will always help you if you have any questions. As you walk about and then go up the stairs you could even imagine how you would feel if you were a pin factory worker.

It is not really surprising to know that ghostly goings on have been experienced in this museum and not so long ago either. A young man working there now told me a very interesting story, although he said he was not too happy about it at the time and freely admits he felt very scared.

One morning the young custodian, Paul, arrived at nine o'clock in good time for work. He was the first one to arrive and opened up the premises just as he had done many times previously. This time it was to be different. He followed the usual procedures and made his way up the stairs. The stairs creaked, but that is perfectly normal and to be expected in such an old building.

Paul reached the place where the pin factory children used to work. Then passed by to the section of old farming equipment. As he stood there, just behind him, the large wooden wheel strongly made and about four feet in diameter turned. Three times to the left and then three times to the right it creaked and rolled. Quickly turning the man was mesmerised, rooted to the spot. He knew he was completely alone. He knew no one had been anywhere near the wheel. It was too heavy and too large to turn without a strong hand to guide it. Shaking with fear he ran down the stairs to the front entrance.

What was it that caused the wheel to turn? We will never know, but perhaps it was the playful ghost of a small pin factory worker. Perhaps wanting to play a trick and be noticed.

The Hasty Retreat

The previous story is not the only incident experienced by the staff there. A different custodian at the museum said that one day he experienced an equally mysterious incident.

Michael was quietly sitting behind his desk in the impressive front entrance. It was a rainy day in winter with not too many visitors. He was startled to see a woman rushing down the stairs, quickly putting on her raincoat to rush out of the building in haste. The man wondered if there was a problem or if there was anything he could do to help. The lady looked very red and flustered and speaking to him insisted that she had seen a ghost. She said it was that of a man dressed up like a woman. Trying to calm the visitor the man tried to ask the lady more details, but she would not stop. Perhaps it had been the figure of a monk. Perhaps the lady had been completely mistaken. Who can say?

Strange Knocking in 1762

The Gloucester Journal in 1762 was by today's standards rather dull for the reader. It was full of small print with information written in a manner which would not be acceptable today. Mr Raikes must have been quite impressed by the following story to include it in his newspaper.

For some time past a great knocking has been heard in the home of a parish clerk, to the great terror of the family. Four gentlemen sat up all night, one of which was a clergyman, trying to discover the meaning of it.

A knocking and scratching came from under the bed of the two children. This was the only place in the house that seemed to be haunted. The child claimed to have seen the ghost of a woman. It was a very bright figure. The man of the house had also seen the spectre. Two years previously a neighbour had also had the same experience.

The man said, 'that in coming out of the kitchen he saw a light on the stairs, and upon looking up saw a bright shining figure of a woman with a bright light shining from it, by which he saw through a window into the nearby Charity school and saw the dial on the school clock.' He stated that many other particulars were related, and two or three clergymen were again prepared to sit up through the night in order to put the troubled spirit to rest.

On enquiry into the truth of this very terrible story we are informed by the wife of the parish clerk, that the thing is an absolute fact, nor was there any room to doubt it. It was said that the poor creature spoke with tears in her eyes. An abundance of people flock hourly to the place in order to enquire the particulars of it. Numbers, however, are actually very incredulous, as to betray a suspicion that there is some deception in the affair, and that it ought to be properly scrutinised.

For our part as we are wonderful believers of stories of this kind, we thought it our duty to do all we could in it, by laying the above anecdotes before the public; and cannot but greatly applaud the very laudable zeal of the truly learned Fraternity of Ballad writers, who we hear are going to perpetuate the memory of this very extraordinary phenomenon, by recording it in their own immortal productions.

We must conclude that the ghost was put to rest as we can find no mention of a ballad or production about this experience.

The Eccentric Millionaire

'One of the Richest Commoners in England', described Jemmy Wood of Gloucester.

How could such a rich man become a drab badly dressed old man, with such an appearance that strangers in London took him to be a pauper?

Robert Raikes worshipped at St Mary de Crypt and so did Jemmy Wood. They shared the same faith but not the same ideals. The two men would nod at the early morning cathedral service on a Sunday morning. Robert Raikes would be there followed by his Sunday School ragamuffins. Robert would give the children sweetmeats and coins from his pocket but Jemmy Wood would give nothing away in spite of his vast wealth.

James Wood was born on the 7 October 1756 and died eighty years later in April 1836. The family home was at Brookthorpe and at 12 years of age he went to King's School, Gloucester where he was a good scholar with a neat hand at writing. The sadness was his appearance, his nose was very large, and hooked almost down to his chin said some folk, and of course he suffered for it.

He fell in love once, and was sadly rejected, a terrible blow to James who must have realised he would always be

Gloucester Old Bank

a laughing stock. His two sisters died at an early age which caused a further sadness to James. He was also well aware of the ridicule that followed him, perhaps that is why he was so mean with his money.

The Gloucester Old Bank, as the small family firm was known, became the place where James learnt all his business skills. James also owned a haberdashery shop. This was left to him by his cousin Anthony Ellis. This man must also have been a hoarder of money as a ton of old copper coins were found in the cellar of the shop when Anthony died.

James was also an undertaker and was often seen to be weeping at funerals. It was later discovered that James kept a diary of all the notable people who died in the city. Their names were written in his beautiful neat slanted handwriting. He was also very interested in the goings on of royalty and in this same notebook wrote a long page of his impressions when the young Victoria came to Gloucester.

James would make his way to work in Westgate Street via the Docks. As he went along he would search for lumps of coal and put them into his pocket. Later the coal would be taken from his pocket and used to keep the fire burning in his shop.

He would pick up turnips from the fields, and one day was taken to task by a man of the law. When James pointed out that in fact he owned the land and let it out to the farmer, James was left to go on his way.

James would often beg a lift rather than pay money. One day he even waved down a hearse and was happy to take a ride in it. James hated to spend money on clothes, and when it was necessary to travel to London on business, his manservant begged him to buy decent clothes fearing they would be refused accommodation in the London inns.

When James wanted to deposit large sums of money in the London banks he persuaded a local business man, a Mr Husbands who owned a clothier's business at The Cross, to take it for him when he went to the city for the latest cloths. This saved a great deal of money which would have been spent on postage and security.

Lottery Tickets in Gloucester

The Government began a state lottery in order to finance the Napoleonic war and Jemmy Wood was licensed to sell lottery tickets, naturally he made a handsome profit on this deal, and the Government found the money to fight the battle. In 1826 lotteries were abolished by the law.

When James Wood died after a short and sudden illness there was a great fuss about his will. Rumours concerning his demise were heard all over the city. Many questions were asked which were never answered. Papers were found which were declared not to be full and proper wills. It was suggested that forgeries had been made, and that codicils had been burnt. Often in his lifetime he said he would do a lot for Old Gloucester. A Mr Chadbourn confessed in court that he had burnt certain papers soon after the old man had died, but claimed they had been old lottery tickets. Many people made claims on the money. The legal profession stepped in to fight different battles. The years went on and Lord Lyndhurst ruled against the executors. The fortune which James Wood had so carefully accumulated quickly diminished. The pockets of the solicitors were lined with his money as the dispute went on. His plans to leave money for a new canal, a new hospital or other good works for the poor came to nothing.

What a shame he had not spent some of his fortune on his own pleasure in his lifetime. No one profited from his mean ways. Money brought no happiness to this Gloucester man. Now, as you pass McDonalds, if you look on the wall you can see a plaque where the original Bank once stood. Jemmy Wood the first banker in Gloucester would surely have been pleased to see The Bank of England make its home just by the Gloucester Docks which he used to pass each day.

THE NINETEENTH CENTURY

The Helpful Ghost

Education for everyone eventually arrived in Gloucester.
The Archdeacon School in Clare Street was known as The
Ragged School of the city. This was the school where
children were able to leave their inadequate homes behind
and begin to learn to read and do sums. A further tribute to
the work begun by Robert Raikes.

The area around Clare Street was at the time full of tiny
houses built close to each other. Summer evenings would
be spent with mothers chatting on the doorstep and the
children tumbling into the narrow streets with their games
and laughter. Sometimes wooden hoops would spin along
the paving stones, tops would spin and dice would roll.
Fathers lucky enough to have a few pence in their pocket
would make their way to one of the many pubs, meet their
friends and often return home much the worse for drink.
Children would know that they had to be indoors before
the men made their noisy way home. A beating could be
the reward for a child still around when Dad came home.
All these things were taking place around the time in 1852
when Archdeacon School opened.

The school in Clare Street soon became popular and even
today some remember their schooldays there. The place is
no longer a school and Donald Jones only knew the fine
building when he went to repair a window at five o'clock
one evening in 1979. Mr Jones used to work for Gloucestershire Council as a glazier and was keen to tell me what

happened to him. He had a message to go to the former school in Clare Street as a window was broken and needed to be replaced as soon as possible. It was nearly time to pack up and go home but Mr Jones thought he could just about get the job done in time. He approached the front entrance and stepped inside the door, just a routine task to be completed quickly. The place was quiet and empty except for a man sitting on a chair. Donald asked the man where he could find the caretaker and the man obligingly pointed his finger to the direction of the stairs. Mr Jones found Marj the caretaker who was pleased to see him arrive so quickly. 'How did you know where to find me?' she asked. Donald replied that the man downstairs had shown him where to go. 'Oh you must have seen our ghost,' replied Marj quite undisturbed. 'There is no one else in the building.' The caretaker went on to tell him that there were many unexplained things regularly taking place in the building. A schoolteacher who had been well loved by the children in his care had one day accidently fallen down the stairs. He was helped into the headmaster's study which at that time was a small room close to the staircase. Before anything could be done to help the poor man he died. Since that time his ghost had been seen allegedly even by the children in a class. Marj said that lights had been seen to go on and off and toilet doors had been locked from the inside. Even local police had been called one night because of lights in the building. Nothing was found. Other staff had felt a push in the back. Decorators who had left equipment in the small locked room whilst away for a lunch break had returned to find paint splashed over the walls.

We hope by now the strange happenings have ceased but I feel obliged to say that whilst Rosemary Harvey my colleague has been telling groups of people about the story, the security light outside the school has come on, even though some way off. Strange indeed.

James Henry Frowde, Champion Clown

Everywhere that Jim the Clown performed audiences were delighted and amused to the point of near hysterics. His antics as a contortionist entertained audiences all over the West country. Children and adults flocked to see his show.

Jim was one of four children and adored his mother who tragically died when he was only six years of age. The last time she spoke to her little family was when she read the Bible to them and reminded them of the time when Jesus was asked who was greatest in the Kingdom of Heaven. His reply came when he placed before him a small child. Jim never forgot his mother or her message, and for some time after he had an unhappy time with bullying teachers and a very strict upbringing. He tried to run away from home when he was only ten, taking with him his Bible and a picture of a small dog. This attempted escape was unsuccessful, but later when Jim was fifteen he met up with his grandfather who was performing in a visiting circus. Jim begged to be allowed to join the family of circus entertainers and was determined to make it his life. He loved the animals especially the dogs and horses.

Jim went along and soon developed his own act as a clown. In August 1852 Henglers Colossal Hippodrome and National Circus visited Gloucester. The main attraction was Jim Frowde. Cheltenham, Tewkesbury, Stroud, Malvern, Monmouth, and all the South of England including Exeter were lucky enough to see the clown, and everywhere he went Jim was applauded with tremendous enthusiasm. In the Cheltenham newspaper it was written 'We feel pleased to hear that his conduct in private life has attracted as much honour and justice as his work in the ring.' Another newspaper said that he was a wise man who played the fool. He was the number one performing clown.

Tragedy again befell our clown when his young wife Elizabeth and baby died. Jim hid his sadness from his audience and continued to delight the crowds leaving his

personal life behind him. Years later Jim met Susan Mary,
and they married. As a family man Jim decided to leave the
travelling life of the circus behind him. He brought
property in Newent and became a farmer.

Jim never forgot his clowning days and continued to
make everyone laugh with his instant humour and quick
wit. He was a Christian and his good knowledge of the
scriptures helped him when he became a lay preacher.
Some people were shocked by his jolly manner, but others
were deeply touched by his words and sincerity. They
loved to hear his stories and he was very popular. After
living in Newent Jim settled in College Green. He loved the
cathedral and was always there. Later he moved to a house
next door to the Folk Museum. This was his last home and
when he died his funeral service was held at St Mary de
Lode.

It takes a wise man to be a fool.

Bishop Ellicott and Palace of Gloucester

We would like to take you on our Step Back in Time tour
to Millers Green, a pleasant place to stand and reminisce.
If the nearby stones could talk they would tell you exciting
and unbelievable stories of days now gone. Nearby is the
old Bishop's Palace and I will tell you a bit about Charles
John Ellicott, Bishop of Gloucester.

1872 was a time when Gloucester was a grand cathedral
city entertaining many members of high society who lived
in the county of Gloucestershire. It was noted by High
Sheriff Dearman Birchall of Bowden Hall that a ball held in
Gloucester at that time was a very grand affair with many
lovely ladies present. He did however complain that the
floor was rough and there were not enough stewards.

Names mentioned at the ball were Gambier Parry of
Highnam Court, Mrs St John Ackers of Prinknash Hall,
W. Hyett of Painswick House, Mrs and Miss Somerset,
cousin of the Duke of Beaufort, Curtis Hayward of Quedgley

Bishop Ellicott

to name but a few. The wife of the bishop was also present. No doubt the bishop had made a suitable excuse as he was not a lover of parties. Mrs Ellicott enjoyed society dinners and had a sharp wit which she sometimes used unkindly. One evening in secret she described a dear young lady named Miss Summer as having the orifices of her nose so marked that one could almost see her brain working.

Mrs Ellicott herself was sometimes the target of amusing gossip. The dean one day at table jokingly said that the wife of the bishop kissed their mastiff dog more heartily then he guessed she kissed the bishop.

In September 1870 the Prince and Princess Christian visited Gloucester for the Three Choirs Festival and the bishop and Mrs Ellicott were pleased to entertain them at the Palace in Gloucester where lunch was provided. Princess Christian was the daughter of Queen Victoria and she married Prince Christian of Schleswig-Holstein in 1866. She was 24 in 1870. The German prince was described later by Dearman Birchall as being light haired but elderly looking, with a balding head, a cold expression with restless eyebrows and a dissatisfied look. The princess however, was an attractive and good-tempered looking girl, wearing a pretty mauve dress with a white flowered bonnet to match. The princess was surprisingly described as speaking with a foreign accent.

The princess sat with the bishop in the middle of the table and she spoke of her love of the music and songs of Mendelsson. She told the bishop and the present company at table that Prince Albert, her father, enjoyed the music by this composer, and had passed on this pleasure to her.

The meal was finished and after a suitable time had passed a royal procession was formed. The party proceeded to the cathedral. It was noted that during the service the Prince Schleswig-Holstein passed a coin to the princess to be given for the collection. This she placed in her glove.

After the service the bishop and Mrs Ellicott led the royal couple followed by the other guests to the Gloucester Palace gardens, where tables were laid with ice and sweets.

Fruit of every delicious colour was on offer. Another table provided tea and coffee. It was said that nothing could have been prettier than the sight of the lawn filled with so many brilliant dresses and gay flowers. The air was filled with animated conversation.

Winter in Gloucester, 1873

1 January 1873 was a day for hunting. It was a tradition in those days enjoyed by all the classes. The gentlemen and farmers with horses rode to the hunt and they would be followed on foot by all manner of people with dogs and children enjoying a day out in the countryside.

This was a hazardous sport. On such a winter's day Miss Ellicott, daughter of the Bishop of Gloucester, set off to ride with the hunt. Miss Ellicott had a fall on this January day whilst riding at Hatherley. She struck her head, injuring her ear which was left hanging by the skin. The lady was rushed in a Spring cart to the Palace and the local doctor was sent for. It took him twenty minutes to sew up the ear. It must have been incredibly painful for the poor girl. Compensation was to follow the incident in the form of Mr Travers who upon seeing the accident followed the cart back to Gloucester, and overcome with compassion proposed to Miss Ellicott. We hope he did not regret his impulsive actions.

Bishop Ellicott had many social occasions to attend but was nonetheless sincere when preforming his spiritual duties. 22 December came along and the bishop had promised to preach the sermon at the church in Upton. The day proved to be a bad one as far as the weather was concerned. The frost and snow were severe but this did not prevent the bishop from preaching. He walked from the Palace in Gloucester to Upton and attended both the morning and evening service.

The bishop and Mrs Ellicott gave many dinners at their home in the Palace which was close to the great cathedral. The couple were known for their hospitality, and the conversation was entertaining and various. Maids would wait at table scurrying to and fro providing the guests with everything they needed, and at the same time enjoying little snippets of gossip. After the meal was finished the gentlemen would retire to the billiard room. It is said the table was quite small and it was not difficult to beat the bishop at this game.

The Frightened Curate

It was a cold January evening in 1872 when, according to a diary kept by Dearman Birchall of Bowden Hall, the bishop told his dinner guests one of his ghost stories. The meal had gone well and everyone at table was feeling warm inside, and ready to leave when the bishop began to talk about one of his favourite rectors who shall be nameless. The bishop was a good looking gentleman as he sat at the table, his distinguished features looking their best, his white curling hair shining in the light of the candles.

It was not the only ghost story told that evening, but it was the only one recorded, so it must have been of consequence. The bishop was inconvenienced by a bad seasonal cold, but this did not affect the telling of his simple and sincere story.

The bishop was approached one day by a rector. The poor man was most distressed and begged for a meeting with the bishop in order to divulge his problem in private. The appointment was duly made. The door opened and the nervous man entered into the bishop's study. Endeavouring to make the man feel at ease the bishop offered the rector a seat. The man perched on the edge of the high-backed dark-stained chair and began to talk. He stuttered in his embarrassment, but encouraged by the kindly bishop he began to speak. 'I am afraid I am obliged to resign, Bishop, I have thought out the situation and I can think of no solution. I do not wish to appear ridiculous, but the fact is I have a ghost at the Vicarage and there is no way she will leave me alone.

'I am obliged to use the study my Lord, to read my books and then write out my sermon for the next week. There is no other room suitable for this task. I like to do this on a

Thursday evening. This seems to be the most convenient time. I then have time, if necessary, to make any alterations to my sermon or indeed change the subject should any last minute occurrence deem it necessary.'

'Yes,' replied the bishop. 'Do get down to the point, I am not a stranger to spiritual matters.'

'The fact is I sit down, get out my pen, paper and begin to pray for guidance to write a good sermon when this woman appears. She is transparent, dressed in blue, and stands in front of my desk, just looking at me. It has not happened just the once. In fact she seems to be coming more frequently if anything. It must be me. I must be unfit for my job. I shall be obliged to resign. It is the only way out. You must think me out of my mind telling you such a story.'

His lordship, the bishop, was still quiet and prepared to give the rector his understanding, he replied. 'I am not prepared to doubt that there may be troubled spirits who cannot rest and force themselves on the presence of the living. Have you courage, yes, then I counsel you to meet and address her with words of sympathy and kindness and offer to pray for her. While speaking the thought came to his mind – sympathy is what she wants, yes sympathy. Convey this to her. She will not come again.'

The rector thanked Bishop Ellicott for his patience and understanding. He went home and the next time he sat down to write his sermon he squarely faced the ghostly spirit. He smiled and promised to pray for her soul. He told her that her problems in this world were over. The loving arms of our Lord Jesus were waiting for her.

He was never troubled again, and continued to minister to his flock in a calm and untroubled way.

It is good to remember Bishop Ellicott and his wisdom.

THE TWENTIETH CENTURY

A Scotsman in Gloucester

Should you visit St John's Lane in Gloucester you will find yourself outside the office of *The Citizen* the local newspaper. Look up and take note of the large hanging memorial of Robert Raikes portraying his head and shoulders. I am told that even now it is a custom for present employees of the paper to look up and say 'Good Morning' to the boss.

Editors have come and gone since the days of Mr Raikes, but there is one that is still remembered by the senior staff of the newspaper. Had it not been for the strange experience of a lady publisher named Victoria I would never have heard about Mr Geoffrey J.J. Robertson.

Victoria turned into St John's Lane and stopped very suddenly, 'I can smell tobacco smoke,' she said. We carried on walking but Victoria remained stock still. It was mid-morning and a very ordinary day, not really the time to expect anything strange to take place. 'I can, I can, I can definitely smell the smell of a cigar,' she insisted, remaining rooted to the spot. 'It is very strong, a cigar, surely you can smell it too?' Just as adamant, we said we could not smell a thing. Victoria said that standing in just the one spot she could smell the aroma of an expensive cigar. If she moved away the smell disappeared but it was definitely a cigar smell. A smell from times now past. As she was so positive, we could not doubt her, and we too wondered if there was a reason for this strange aroma.

At a later date I casually mentioned this strange experi-

52

ence to Mr David Browne the features editor of the newspaper who visibly paled at the story. 'It must surely have been G.J.J. Robertson,' he said.

Mr G.J.J. Robertson

A great man and a character known by everyone in the city. G.J.J.R. as he was known was the editor in the '50s and '60s. A Scotsman larger than life he would enter the offices and if anything was amiss the sound of loud Scottish vituperation would fill the air accompanied by the strong smell of smoke. Mr Robertson would invariably be seen with a pipe or cigar in his mouth, smoked in true Scottish fashion. He was a patriotic exile. If ever a vagrant Scotsman was in Gloucester, it was accepted that he only had to present himself to G.J.J.R. in order to be rewarded with half a crown and sent on his way with a kind word. Office workers soon became accustomed to rubbing shoulders with itinerants.

The editor was an accomplished after dinner speaker and his favourite party trick would be to real off misquotes from his own newspaper much to the amusement and delight of his fellow guests. Mr Robertson knew nearly everyone in the city and made it his business to always be out and about. He was a great ambassador of *The Citizen* newspaper and was always socially vociferous. He was a governor of King's School and keen to help in whatever way he could.

In the year 1955 when the Queen visited the cloisters and just before she made her way to the historic Chapter House, Mr Robertson was present, as David Leach, head boy of the King's School, greeted the Queen in Latin. The event was well reported in the paper and told of the Queen going on to the Wagon Works and the Hospital.

The Gloucester Scottish Society was also proud to have G.J.J.R. in their midst and members never grew tired of the tales he had to tell.

Perhaps as a former newspaper editor G.J.J. Robertson felt obliged to make his presence felt to a fellow publisher.

Around the Cathedral

St Michael's Gate also known as Pilgrim's Gate is an interesting porchway which leads from the Cathedral Close into a lane named College Court. It is said that the gate was known as the Pilgrim's Gate because that was the entrance used by weary travellers coming from Westgate Street and then into the cathedral. Their muddy boots and dusty clothes were not appreciated in the main entrance so they went through the porch and were guided into the cathedral by the small side gate.

As they came in the door a monk would be there to lead the way. The pilgrims would take a candle and light it then reverently approach the tomb of Edward II. The monk in charge of the group would give them a tour around the cathedral and they would then be able to join in the next service, pray to God and give thanks for their safe arrival. After the cathedral visit they would go to the inn of their choice, have a rest, clean themselves up as best they could, then food and beer would be taken and the visit enjoyed.

The Pilgrim's Gate Apparition

With all this history around, is it any wonder that now and again unexplained sightings are reported?

Around the year 1950 a young lady named Peggy Tether worked for Scott Fowler the solicitor. The business was operated from a house situated just inside The Close near to the Pilgrim's Gate. Peggy has since married and now lives in Bristol. Gloucester is now only a place to visit relatives who are still living there. At the time of the sighting Peggy was a young secretary. Evening In Paris was the favourite perfume. Girls wore wide waspie elastic belts. Circular cotton skirts were worn on top of stiff nylon waist slips. It was the height of fashion. Boys plastered Brylcreem on their hair and Dennis Compton, the cricketer, was a hero. Diana Dors from Swindon was the glamourous film star whose name was on everybody's lips. None of this affected

Peggy very much as she worked away in her office. The morning began sharply at nine o'clock and finished promptly at five-thirty. A polite telephone manner was essential and O.K. was strictly forbidden as a phrase to be used to clients.

A solicitor's practice in the 1950s was a lot more difficult than now as far as paperwork was concerned. This was the time before word processors and disks. A secretary was expected to be an efficient shorthand typist, and accurate with the filing. Paperwork was stored in piles waiting for the day when it was necessary to check back on figures, facts, wills, and litigation, even though the years had made the paper brown and the texture crisp.

Solicitors needed a lot of storage space to accommodate the papers, and a document filed away under the wrong heading could cause hours of frustration. Basement rooms were ideal for storage. Spiders and dust would fly as juniors were sent on errands to collect old documents.

The basement at Peggy Tether's place of employment was well used for this purpose. One such afternoon she was asked to go to the cellar and re-organise the filing and redeem a document. Peggy sat there absorbed by her task, when looking up she saw a lady sitting still and watching her. The woman seemed quite comfortable and wore a long black dress with a white collar and a cap on her head. Peggy gasped and was almost transfixed. It seemed a long pause, but on reflection was only a few seconds. Peggy ran upstairs to tell her story, but as she had forgotten the document she had to return almost immediately. The cellar was completely quiet and deserted, but she still remembers the company she had that day. Was it a weary pilgrim resting after a long journey, or perhaps someone who had lived once in a house on that site? We will never know.

Crews in the Close

The summer of 1994 saw many new and unfamiliar faces in the Close of the cathedral. Faces that were unfamiliar in our city but well known, indeed very well known, on the

Gloucester Cathedral

cinema and TV screen. *The Choir* was here. That is *The Choir* as written by Joanna Trollope the talented author who lives nearby in the Cotswolds. Apparently Joanna visited the cathedral one day and was inspired to write the first chapter of the book.

Gloucester people adapted to the sight of film crews appearing in the main streets, bogus bishops made purchases in local bookshops during their break, and Jane Asher popped into Pilgrim's Walk bakery for her croissants. James Fox or Will as his mother still calls him, strolled down the street. David Warner looking more like a bishop than any I have seen was around. Nicholas Farrell and Cathryn Harrison were free to be seen together without causing any gossip in the Close. Rosemary Harvey and myself whilst walking around the outside of the cathedral on our Step Back in Time Tours were pleased to tell people of the history of the city and the ghosts that reputedly are still around. We never knew what to expect those fine summer evenings when most of the filming was taking place. One night we were fortunate enough to see the cathedral blazing with light and even the grass outside was bright as filming continued for twenty-four hours in order to get the cathedral and the unusually busy Close isolated for the shots.

I was walking with the visitors telling them about a man from Bournemouth who had telephoned me one Saturday morning concerning the ghost of a monk he had witnessed whilst walking in Gloucester. He insisted that a door at the side of the cathedral had remained closed whilst a ghostly monk had walked right out of the place and crossed the path close by him. I was pointing mysteriously to this door when just at that moment it slowly opened and out came a film technician carrying equipment. The poor man was dumbstruck to encounter a group of people who burst into laughter as he emerged.

It was the same night that I told them about a woman named Liz, one of the wonderful band of ladies who give their services so freely in order to help maintain the cathedral. She had offered to help out with a bit of spring cleaning, and was working on an elaborate marble tomb. In her hand she carried a small pot full of powder to polish the marble surface. She was on her knees behind the tomb and as time went by her knees became stiff and uncomfortable. Slowly she rose, stretching her legs and raising her arms above her head, at the same time giving out a loud yawn. An Italian tourist who, unknown to Liz, had been examining the tomb from the other side gave a terrified scream. The lady trying to calm the man began to explain her reason for being there. Alas the poor man did not understand English and stepped back in horror. He then threw a handful of coins into her pot of cleaning powder and rushed out of the cathedral.

Should you ever meet an Italian who swears he has seen a ghost in Gloucester I am afraid this time you must not believe him.

Ladies who help in the cathedral are not all surprised at strange stories concerning the cathedral. They know and love the place and feel the same sense of belonging as Gloucester people before them. If a monk feels the need to sometimes return they understand. A lady in the bookshop just by the entrance, which now stands on the spot where the martyred Bishop Hooper once held his services, said that she herself had glanced down the aisle from her place behind the counter and had seen the figure of a diminutive monk walking towards the entrance. One minute he was there and the next he had disappeared. A trick of the light, or a genuine experience. Who is to say?

✦✦

Freddy Grisewood and his Gloucester Experience
✦ ✦ ✦ ✦ ✦ ✦ ✦ ✦ ✦   ✦ ✦ ✦ ✦ ✦ ✦ ✦ ✦ ✦ ✦ ✦ ✦ ✦ ✦ ✦ ✦ ✦ ✦ ✦

The famous BBC Broadcaster Freddy Grisewood was a name well known to every radio listener during the '50s and '60s. He was a West country celebrity who, when was not in London or away working on location, lived in Daylesford, near Moreton-in-Marsh. Freddy was a popular

West Country figure able to relate to anyone he met, be it prince or pauper. His quick wit and sharp comments made him an invaluable member of the interviewing team based in Broadcasting House.

Any Questions was one of the popular programmes hosted by Freddy. There was also *Gardener's Question Time*. Both programmes are still regular radio favourites. Listeners from that era will also remember *Down Your Way* when Freddy visited various places all over the country picking out the most important spots of interest and also interviewing local characters who would tell you what to expect should you visit the spots mentioned. It was very easy listening and widely appreciated by the public.

Sheila Goodwin told me about an odd confrontation Freddy had when he visited Gloucester for the *Down Your Way* programme. The great cathedral was then, and still is, the most important tourist attraction. Naturally enough Freddy wanted to tell listeners about the place, hoping to give them the opportunity of first hand knowledge, should they ever wish to visit it for themselves.

The cloisters seemed ideally situated for the recording team. Interviews were organised with Freddy and the technicians set up the basic but adequate equipment used at that time. Things did not proceed smoothly however for as soon as Freddy stepped into the cloisters he claimed to feel invisible hands clutching at him around his throat. In front of the technicians he staggered about and grabbed at his neck. At first it seemed amusing to the waiting crew, but to Freddy the experience was so unpleasant that he insisted on moving all the gear away from the cloisters and doing the broadcast inside the main cathedral church.

Sheila said that even more strangely some years later, long after the incident, Freddy returned to Gloucester Cathedral as a private tourist. He approached the cloisters, only to be confronted by the same nasty experience. Unseen hands again clutched at him. He retreated and was content to restrict his visit to the cathedral.

I cannot think that this incident could have been in any

way connected with the gentle monks of St Peter. Perhaps it was something to do with the aggressive soldiers of Oliver Cromwell, who during the Civil War and in contempt of the established church used the cloisters as a place in which to tether their horses. I have never heard of anyone else experiencing anything but peace and calm in this beautiful place.

The Monks

As we walk around the cloisters of the great cathedral every step we take reminds us of the monks who worshipped and worked around the abbey. How cold they must have been as they washed at the water troughs, still seen at the far end of the cloisters. Hygiene was not quite so meticulous then. The monks would have a quick sluice and then make a rapid dash across to the opposite cloister wall where the towels for drying would be hung against the kitchen wall for warmth. The water would be provided from a well from the diverted River Twyver, and the sewerage would flow to the River Severn. Monasteries were then built by rivers as a necessity, not just a whim for would-be fishermen.

The monks lived in the cloisters. Thick leather curtains would be hung in winter to keep out the draughts, but there was no heating except in the warming room which they would rush to from time to time to stop the numbness in their bones. Then back again to the cold. As the monks got older they must have suffered terribly from rheumatism and chest complaints. The habits they wore were made from fine local wool, and helped keep out the cold. Feet would be wrapped around with straw in winter and bound with twine. Hands would be thrust into the loose sleeves of their gowns as they made their way to worship in the early hours of the morning. Many of the chants they sang are still used by the cathedral choir boys today. They used music and art as gifts from God. The monks who ministered to the sick must have been very busy making potions for coughs and colds and also constipation. The diet they ate was very basic and did not include a variety of fruit and fresh vegetables. Bodily ailments were frequent and unpleasant.

We can still see the spot where the herb garden or herbarium was kept as the garden of the Little Cloister. The monastic infirmary was the best hospital around then, and men of the city would save any money they could in order to spend their last years being tended by the gentle monks. Food was plentiful for the monastery and a tenth of all the venison from the Forest of Dean was their right. Fish too was eaten regularly. Almsgiving for the poor was part of the Benedictine rule, and after every evening meal food for the poor was available just outside the cathedral gate.

In the cloisters we can see the little carrels built to catch the daylight. Here the monks would work at their manuscripts, some of the beautiful books they completed were the product of a lifetime's work. The delicate gold plated calligraphy was produced to perfection. Sometimes the monks would suck their brushes. They did not realise then that this could lead to lead poisoning, which meant a painful death. A local calligrapher, Joy Annis, told me an amusing story about the manner in which monks used gesso, which is a plaster base beneath the gold lettering. The substance made was found to bubble but a monk discovered that if ear wax was added to the mixture no bubbles formed.

The *Scriptorium* would usually, as in our own cathedral cloister, be located near to the library and also the warming room. A goose quill would be used for the writing, the feather selected from among the five best wing quills of a large bird. The feather would be soaked for softening and then dried with hard sand, then cut to form a point. The completed books would be the result of teamwork. First of all the parchment had to be made and then finished in the tanning yard.

Scribes would prepare the page by either ruling lines or pricking out dots. Another monk would lay the gesso and then the gilder would put on the gold. Others would do the painting or writing. If a monk became sick or died the work would be carried on. One twelfth century monk wrote that if anyone thought the task to be a simple one . . . 'Let me tell you that it destroys your eye sight, bends your spine, squeezes your stomach and your sides, pinches your lower back and makes your whole body ache.'

The monks were pleased to sup the small beer they brewed. It must have helped a little to keep out the cold.

We cannot be surprised that from time to time people claim to catch a glimpse of a monk. Whilst walking around the cloisters, especially in the evening we have been told that some people have experienced the smell of beer. This was described in detail as a meady light sort of beer, giving out a sweet smell of hops. The odour apparently comes and then disappears in wafts. Another man said he has seen a vision of small children from another age running around the cloisters and then disappearing.

The cloisters were wonderful. In fact I think they are the most peaceful place to visit within the city of Gloucester. The gardens are good to relax in, and one's thoughts are taken back to another age in no time at all.

Miracle at the High Altar

In our present busy lives the mention of a miracle is met with sceptism but in St Peters Abbey in the twelfth century the people of Gloucester claimed to have witnessed a great life saving miracle.

The Bishop of Worcester was celebrating mass at the high altar. It must have been a special service as there were other ministers present and a full choir of monks with a multitude of people of both sexes. It was recorded at that time that, just as the service was coming to an end, the large high tower of the church collapsed. It is said that the crash and shock as the foundation fell down suddenly was so great that the earth shook in such a manner that was never before seen or heard. The noise was tremendous. The ministers serving at the altar fled in fear of their life. The monks in the choir scattered running with their hands about their ears. Others stood transfixed in horror expecting the whole abbey to collapse, and certain death their way out of this life. Dust flew everywhere with mortar, masonry stones, and timber in ruin.

As everyone in the abbey grew quiet, standing in shocked expectation, their eyes became accustomed to the thick dust in the air. They could again see what had happened amidst the destruction and debris. In spite of the hurried exit of the choir and other clergy, the bishop stood quietly, alone and still. He remained in this attitude of fixed devotion seemingly oblivious to the disaster that had just taken place. Even though the tower had been at the Western part of the church no one in the building had suffered harm. 'It was as if it had been the pious disposition of the Saviour,' it was stated at that time, and everyone present that day agreed that indeed a miracle had taken place.

Services in the cathedral now tend to be much quieter and uneventful.

◆◆

The Small Boy in the Fireplace

◆ ◆

In Cathedral Close many lovely houses stand. Church House is beautiful and inside the magnificent staircases tell of times now past. The gabled front exterior was originally built in the thirteenth century. It was the house which was used by the abbot to entertain his royal and otherwise important guests. The former Abbot's Hall is now divided into two large rooms. They are still used for various special occasions, sometimes wedding receptions are held there with the catering done by the restaurant housed within the cathedral buildings.

One room is named the Laud Room and it has Jacobean wood panelled walls. The other room is called the Henry Room with an attractive ceiling. Henry VIII and Anne

Boleyn were entertained here when they visited Gloucester, and it is said they were well pleased with the welcome they received. They would certainly have had the best of Gloucestershire food and drink. Venison from the forest, game birds, and pigs stuffed with lemon would have been on the menu. Apples from the nearby orchards and plenty of other fruit, with spices and herbs to enhance the flavour. Wine, mead and ale would have been on the table. Entertainers would have been used with jokers and musicians to keep the party going.

During Elizabethan times, especially in summer when the weather was hot and unwashed bodies were inclined to smell a bit, perfumes and dried flowers were used indoors to disguise the various aromas. Large stone vases were used for flower displays and sometimes guests would wander over to the fireplace as a temporary respite from unpleasantness.

It is the fireplace in the room which stands above the restaurant used by visitors to the cathedral that seems by all accounts to be possibly haunted.

Penny from the restaurant says that the figure of a small boy has been seen moving around the large fireplace. Others claim that the empty fireplace often gives off the beautiful heavy scent of dried flowers. It has also been said that even when the rooms are empty and locked a sound of heavy objects being dragged across the floor and then footsteps have been heard. What a mystery!

GLOUCESTER CONNECTIONS

◆◆
Gloucester and the Bible
◆ ◆ ◆ ◆ ◆ ◆ ◆ ◆ ◆ ◆ ◆ ◆ ◆ ◆ ◆ ◆ ◆ ◆ ◆ ◆ ◆ ◆ ◆ ◆ ◆ ◆ ◆

William Tyndale of Gloucestershire translated the Bible for all to read. It was his one ambition in life. He succeeded and his reward was to be hounded all over Europe and strangled at the stake for his troubles.

William Tyndale sometimes named as Hutchins was born in North Nibley. He went to Oxford when only thirteen years of age and was a brilliant scholar. He was always a rebel and was often in trouble for trying to find out the truth in his own way. Because of this he was at loggerheads with the established church. Hope Costley White the 1950s historian stated that he would go to Gloucester and spend time arguing with the monks there. It is noted that he stood on the place outside the Augustinian monastery now known as College Green and preached. He felt like Bishop Hooper who was martyred at the stake in Gloucester in 1555 believing that the Bible should be the basis of Christian religion. The monks stormed round him in disagreement, it was then considered that the English tongue was far too coarse to be suitable for a translation, which led him to make the vow. 'If God spare my life, I will cause that a boy that driveth the plough shall know more about the Scriptures than you do.'

He began to work on the translation. He used a secret room at the home of a cloth merchant in Monmouth. Soon even that became too dangerous, and he fled to Germany. In 1525 the printing of his translation of the New Testament began in Cologne. His enemies passed on this news to

William Tyndale

Cardinal Wolsey and Henry VIII. He fled again to Worms on the Rhine to complete printing the 6,000 copies.

English travellers in the cloth trade in Germany were persuaded to smuggle copies back to England.

The Bishop of London found a copy and was furious to find Bibles in our vulgar English tongue. He ordered all the books to be sought out and burnt at a great public bonfire which was held in Paul's Cross. William Tyndale did not stop and continued to print further copies. The demand was now increasing and people wanted to know about this New Testament Bible for themselves. Archbishop Wolsey sent his men to Worms and ordered the arrest of William Tyndale who knew and understood the risks he was taking.

Early in the morning on 6 October 1535 when only forty-six years old William Tyndale was taken to the stake. His last words were 'Lord open up the eyes of the King of England'. He was then strangled and his body burned.

Henry VIII misread the will of the people of England. They were angry and wanted to read the Bible for themselves. How did they know whether or not the words were meant for them. They thought there must be something special about the translation or else why would such an educated man die in order to write the book. Three years elapsed and the king decreed that every church should have its own copy of the English Bible. The new version was written by Miles Coverdale who followed Tyndale closely.

On 29 May 1863 high on a hill where all could see, an obelisk was raised at North Nibley. And even later in 1938 a tablet was placed in Westminster Abbey in honour of the brave man who was translator of The Holy Scriptures into the language of the English people.

Now the one remaining copy of the three thousand which were published in 1526 has been taken from its hiding place under lock and key where it remained for two hundred years in Bristol Baptist College, and has been auctioned for the grand sum of one million pounds. The British Library were determined that this one copy should remain in England.

What has this to do with Gloucester? The answer is that in May 1936 a descendant of William Tyndale, namely a Mr Alfred Walter Hitchings of Nottingham left a wonderful bequest to our library in Gloucester. He left his entire collection of over a hundred precious Bibles. There were two copies of the Miles Coverdale translation of 1550, and a Matthews Bible of 1551.

The collection of New Testaments include a copy of the Erasmus New Testament in Latin, 1519, and four copies of the Tyndale Bible. The earliest one published in 1536. The latest in 1553.

Tragedy at Little Sodbury Manor

Little Sodbury Manor lying on the slopes of the Cotswolds was the family home of Sir John Walsh in 1552. It stood just twelve miles from Stinchcombe the home of the Tyndale family.

It was to the Manor House at Sodbury after completing his education at Oxford and then Cambridge that William Tyndale went to work for Sir John Walsh as tutor to his children.

Sir John Walsh was a prominent man at court at one time when he acted as King's Champion at the coronation of Henry VIII. His wife was Anne Poyntz daughter of a prominent Gloucestershire family. The couple's children needed a tutor and Sir John chose William Tyndale for the position. He respected his views and treated him as an equal who shared the table. They would discuss politics and religion well into the night. His wife too would take part in the talks. Maurice was the name of their eldest boy.

A terrible event happened some thirty years later at the Manor House in Little Sodbury during a dreadful thunderstorm when Maurice was sitting at the table with his own family of nine children. Atkyns, the old Gloucester historian, recorded that 'a fiery sulphurous globe came rolling in at the parlour door' and passed out through a window on the other side of the room. One child was killed outright, and the father and six others died within two months.

This remarkable story was confirmed by the will of Maurice Walsh which was made when he was a widower on 7 June 1556 mentioning his nine children; he added a codicil on 21 June, and another on 18 July saying that four daughters and one of his elder sons were dead. The will was proved on 28 September and the third son succeeded to the title and estate.

Chavanage House Hauntings

A few miles outside of Royal Tetbury lies Chavanage House. Just to see it takes your breath away. It is the perfect setting for scenes of a past age. This is an opinion which has been shared by film directors and film stars. The house has been used as a background for many swashbuckling films and even Mr Poirot has solved a problem there.

If you are lucky enough to enter the house it has the added benefit of still being used as a family home. It is not a museum and is all the better for it. Outside is a lovely little Catholic chapel where the family still worship. Local people have also been able to see performances of William Shakespeare plays in the grounds. A perfect setting on a summer evening, and a glass of wine sipped during the interval makes the whole occasion idyllic.

During the Civil war of 1642 Chavanage House was host to many secret meetings. The place was used as a neutral ground away from parliament. Disagreements echoed around the walls. Gloucestershire at that time was a divided county. Some people were loyal Royalists hoping to save Charles I from execution and others were Parliamentarians hoping to enjoy a new government led by Cromwell.

Each county sent two members to parliament, and at the election in 1640 John Dutton was a Royalist and Nathaniel Stephens who lived at Chavanage and supported Parliament was his opponent. At his second attempt of that year Nathaniel Stephens was elected and sent to the House of Commons. During the Siege of Gloucester Nathaniel was instructed by Parliament to be steadfast in his work of persuading the people of Gloucester to hold out and stop the king from taking over the city. This he did.

Eventually the civil war was over and for a while Parliament was in charge of our country. Nathaniel Stephens like many of the people living in Gloucester at that time supported Parliament, but did not hold anything against the king and was not in favour of putting him on trial. Nathaniel wanted to come to terms with the king, but Oliver Cromwell did not want any opposition and insisted that the king should be tried.

There is a story that Oliver Cromwell made a secret personal visit to Chavanage House. He was determined to change Nathaniel's mind. He wanted his support and thought he might make the obstinate man see his side of the dispute. Arguing went on well into the night. A lot of shouting, drinking, and eating would surely have taken place. The room where Cromwell spent the night after the discussions can still be seen at the top of the wooden stairs in the house. It is said that ghostly footsteps have been heard moving around this room, and also on the staircase leading to the room. Perhaps Oliver Cromwell had unfinished business to resolve.

Nathaniel had a cousin in parliament at that time who agreed with him. Edward Stephens of Little Sodbury was the member for Tewkesbury. He too was strongly against a trial for the king, and wrote and published a 'Letter of Advice to Sir Thomas Fairfax'. The letter begged him to prevent the nation from murdering the king.

Charles I was put on trial in 1649 and executed. Nathaniel Stephens was not a member of the court and was not persuaded by Cromwell to betray the king. There were others who were pleased to give evidence and as we know the deed was done. Nathaniel died in 1660. This was the same year that royalty was restored and Charles II took his place on the throne.

The night he died it is said that his shadow left the house in a carriage driven by a headless man who was wearing the king's livery. The carriage made a noisy exit rattling across the cobbled stones in front of the house. Since that day it is said that from time to time the carriage repeats the ride and draws up outside the front entrance of this fine house. Some have claimed to have heard the noise of carriage wheels thundering in haste away from the scene. A strange story. Chavanage House certainly looks mysterious even to this day. I wonder if Hercule Poirot found out what really happened?

✦✦

Bishop John Hooper of Gloucester

✦ ✦

If you have ever been to St Mary's Square and seen the grand memorial to Bishop Hooper, you could not have failed to be impressed. Just to stand there and imagine the sad and terrible end of this brave, stubborn and obstinate man is enough to send shivers down the spine. Bishop Hooper was an unfortunate victim of the religious changes, as were many others. Queen Mary was a staunch Catholic and during her brief reign was bent on doing everything within her power to bring back the Church of Rome to England. The clergy in the land were to support her, and if not, they could expect to feel the consequences.

Mary had suffered greatly because of her father King Henry VIII. Her mother was Queen Catherine, the first and dutiful wife of Henry. Mary was a big disappointment to her father through no fault of her own. He had dearly wanted a son and heir, in fact he was convinced Catherine would have a boy. He later wanted a divorce from Catherine in order to marry Anne Boleyn, but the Pope in Rome would not dissolve the marriage. Henry had put forward to the Pope that as Catherine had been married previously to his dead brother, the marriage must be null and void. The Pope would not consider it, and this is believed to have been the real reason behind the persecution of the Catholic Church in England.

King Henry got his own way, the marriage was dissolved, and the path was clear at last to make Anne his bride. Needless to say Mary was unhappy in her childhood, and blamed it all on her father and his break with Rome. Mary, like her mother, was a devout Roman Catholic, and vowed to do all she could to bring back the Church of Rome. Her younger brother Edward IV was heir to the throne, and Mary was pushed into the background, but all this changed when the young king died. Mary was crowned queen, and from then on was bent on making everyone aware that she was now the one in charge.

Bishop Hooper, the man who had reluctantly agreed to become Bishop of Gloucester and had prophetically chosen as his coat of arms the lamb in the burning bush now became a target of Mary's wrath. 'Bloody Mary', as she became known sent the protestant bishop to jail on a trumped up charge claiming that he owed money to the crown.

Bishop John Hooper was a stubborn man quite prepared to die for his faith. Prison did not weaken his spirit although his body was wracked with rheumatism and disease caused by the privations of his imprisonment. It was ordered that he was to be returned from Newgate Prison, escorted to Gloucester and burnt at the stake as an example.

After two days spent in a house in Westgate Street, Bishop Hooper was led to the pyre, and on 9 February 1555 in front of a crowd of 7,000 people the holy man perished. He was bound with iron hoops. He was not allowed a farewell speech, but this did not prevent him praying. Three bladders of gunpowder were strapped to his body, but John Hooper remained conscious. The fire needed to be lit twice and death was agonising and slow.

A man present later described the scene, 'When he was black in the mouth, his tongue swollen, unable to speak, his lips went on till they were shrunk at the gums. He knocked his breast with his hands, until one of his arms fell off, then fat water and blood dropped from his finger tips. He never stopped praying during this ordeal which lasted half an hour and when his body was finally destroyed his spirit rose and he was finally at peace.'

People watching in the crowd were moved as never before and one blind teenage boy insisted that he held the same beliefs as Bishop Hooper. Others tried to lead the boy away unheeded but his insistence was so great that he too became a martyr and was later burnt.

Shirt of Fire

This story of Bishop Hooper inspired Canon Robin Green-wood of Cathedral Close. He thought up the idea of presenting a play for the people of the city. What a wonderful story. It called out to be turned into a drama.

A man from Ripon named Derek Stevens was commis-sioned to make the story into a drama. Derek became very excited by the task, and soon, after studying his personality through all the history books he read, felt he knew John Hooper personally. Derek as a Yorkshireman sympathised with Hooper's stubborn persistence and his disquieting manner of calling a spade a spade. Hooper believed in cutting out the trimmings and getting down to brass tacks. A man after his own heart.

A magnificent script was completed requiring a cast of over a hundred people. Could it be done? The answer was Yes. Robin Greenwood set about the task of persuading Gloucester people to come forward and offer their serv-ices, however modest, to produce a community play. Locally based English and American insurance groups put the play on a sound financial backing by sponsoring the production cost. It took a year to get the play together and the result was a production which was a great success.

In the great cathedral setting characters from the six-teenth century became alive. The costumes were quite incredible. Local ladies made the clothes insisting that everything was historically correct to the last detail. John Nash was the exacting director, and soon he was guiding bishops, clergy, queens, and princes, not to mention the local poorly clad citizens who lived in Gloucester at that time. I saw a plea in *The Citizen* for players and persuaded my friend, the reluctant Rosemary to join me.

Rehearsals were underway. Rosemary and I were laugh-ing in the background when John Nash pounced on us one evening. 'I have a special part for you two,' he said. What an honour we thought, could this be our big chance for a leading part? Next week we came down to earth. John asked us if we would play two drunken ladies of pleasure. The only light entertainment of the play, we had to enter the cathedral carrying a jug of ale and cackling with drunken laughter.

Eventually everything fitted into place. Rehearsals were mainly held in the Chapter House. We soon became accustomed to wandering around the unlit cloisters in the evenings and we wore our warmest underwear to combat the wintry cold. It was then we appreciated just how cold it must have been for the monks.

The date of the first production was set for 8 November 1990. Tickets were a sell out for the three days and excitement was mounting. The dress rehearsal in the cathedral was a wonderful occasion. We all made our way dressed in our clothes provided by the ladies of the wardrobe waiting for the play to unfold.

The scene was set for Bishop Hooper to make his way from the main cathedral entrance where he would burst through the floodlit doors and walk slowly down the aisle leaning on his bishop's staff. The people of Gloucester would be waiting to see their bishop and receive his blessing for the last time. I was one of the crowd.

This is the moment when I had a very strange experience. The door opened and John Wilson as Bishop Hooper made a dramatic entrance. He silently entered the cathedral. As the bishop drew near we were supposed to bow to him. Up until this moment this had been hard to do and John Nash had urged us to be less wooden in our greeting.

Suddenly I threw myself on the floor greeting the bishop with cries of sadness and grief. I looked up at him and the words *'Deus Pax Volente'*, shot through my head. My grief had been real. Another extra to my right was amazed at my so-called acting. 'Steady on,' she said. 'It's only a rehearsal,' but I was really shaken. I kept the words in my head and as soon as I found a pen I wrote them down. I looked them up at a later date and found that it was Latin for 'The Peace of God be With You', and would have been a blessing used by our Bishop Hooper when he lived in Gloucester.

I have no explanation to offer.

✦✦✦
Westgate Bridge
✦ ✦ ✦ ✦ ✦ ✦ ✦ ✦ ✦ ✦ ✦ ✦ ✦ ✦ ✦ ✦ ✦ ✦ ✦ ✦ ✦ ✦ ✦ ✦ ✦ ✦ ✦ ✦

The Angry Welshmen

Westgate Bridge stood for hundreds of years at the far end of Westgate Street. It was a beautiful construction with fine curved arches spanning the river with a Gate Tower at the city end enabling people to cross from Over into the city. It was the gateway from Gloucester to the Forest of Dean and then the wild and windy hills of Wales. It played an important part in many skirmishes not least of them the Civil War of Gloucester in 1642.

King Charles was sure the people of Gloucester would be loyal and submit to his army of soldiers positioned outside the city walls. He underestimated the feelings of the citizens of the city under the leadership of the young Colonel Massey, a professional and ambitious young soldier. Prince Rupert led a force of six thousand horses after taking Cirencester and approached the city hoping to aid King Charles who was staying at Matson House on the outskirts of Gloucester with his two sons. Colonel Massey swore he would not deliver the city to a foreign prince, meaning Rupert, and no one knew which way the fighting would go.

Lord Herbert from the other side of Gloucester raised a force of two thousand Welshmen. They may have been reluctant but nevertheless they were in no position to refuse. Through lack of strategy on the Royal side Massey was able to work out a crafty plan with Sir William Waller who on 23 March 1643 led an army across the River Severn at Framilode in flat bottomed boats at the dead of night. By means of a pre-arranged plan Sir William Waller who was nicknamed 'William the Conqueror' met up with Colonel Massey and his men at Highnam. The small army camping

Westgate Bridge

at and around Highnam House under Sir Jerome Brett were asleep and taken by surprise. A terrible bloody battle ensued and five hundred men were slain. Before he returned to Gloucester Colonel Massey made sure to raze Highnam House to the ground in case it should be used again by the enemy. Priceless manuscripts written by George Herbert the poet, whose widow had married Sir Robert Cooke, were destroyed in the fire.

Colonel Massey took sixteen humdred prisoners and, in order to demonstrate their success against the Welshmen, the wretched prisoners were marched from the battle. They were dragged along across Westgate Bridge to be greeted by jeering Gloucester men who shouted and baited the sorry soldiers.

Not knowing quite what to do with them Massey led them through the city and they were locked up in Trinity Church and St Mary de Lode which is thought to be the oldest church in the city. The prisoners were fed on turnip tops, cabbage leaves and such food scraps. A few buckets of dirty water from the River Severn was probably given to them too. After five days the doors were unbolted and the bedraggled and wretched men were returned to Westgate Bridge and sent on their way to find a route back home as best they could. It was brought up in Parliament at a sitting the next December that the church of St Mary de Lode in Gloucester had been in a ruinous condition ever since it had been used as a prison for the Welsh.

Some people say that because of what happened in the Civil War in 1643, when Gloucester finally sent King Charles fleeing and on his way to Falmouth in Cornwall there remains a certain feeling of rivalry between the Welsh and the citizens of Gloucester. Now the battles are fought at the Rugby ground in Kingsholm in a more friendly way, but still with intense passion.

St Mary de Lode and the Shipwrecked Priest

St Mary de Lode Church is one of the oldest places of Christian worship in the country. It is exquisitely beautiful and what is more it is a living church with lots of activities going on and members proud and happy to be involved with the past and present history of the building. It is hard to believe that in the notorious rebuilding plans of the sixties serious considerations were made to convert the nave into a church hall. Fortunately through donations and the hard work and protestations of the Vicar W.G. Pritchard who lived in Millers Green, the vicarage at that time, the place was saved.

The church stands on the site of a rather grand Roman house. The tiled floor is still visible beneath the floor and is on view on special occasions. The tiles were bluish grey, red and white when rediscovered in 1978. It is claimed that the Romans living in Gloucester then may well have used the building as a temple and a place of Christian worship.

St Mary de Lode was the Mother church of the whole of

St Mary de Lode

the city at one time and was the only parochial church recorded in Gloucester by the Domesday book. It was constructed in the early days, of Severn river water, wattle and daub. There is also the traditional tale that a Christian King was buried here as long ago as the third century. Robert of Gloucester's chronicle claims that King Lucius of Britain, the first Christian king of England who died just four years after his conversion, was buried in St Mary de Lode Church.

The River Severn would have flowed quite close to the church when it was first built enabling visitors to travel by water and also a means of transporting supplies. Although Gloucester was visited by the Danes in 877, Ethelred ruled in Gloucester later under Alfred the Great and was buried in the parish in 911. With such a great historical background it is almost expected that St Mary de Lode has a ghost story to tell.

In the fourteenth century the priest in charge of St Mary de Lode decided to fulfil a lifelong ambition to go on a pilgrimage to Rome. He promised his anxious flock that he would return in time to celebrate mass on Christmas Eve. The priest set off on what must have been an amazing journey. The dangers and hardships were considerable. He was successful reaching Rome and we hope he was able to see everything he wanted. The priest set off for home determined to keep his promise and be back at St Mary de Lode in time for Christmas. Sadly this was not to be and the poor man was drowned at sea on his return journey. The boat was shipwrecked and all were lost.

After that sad day many people apparently reported that the ghost of the priest troubled the church. It was claimed in a story in *The Citizen* newspaper that at midnight on Christmas Eve a gale of wind swept through the church and the ghost of the absent priest entered the sanctuary of the church. The story goes that many years after this event the vicar at the church decided to help the restless spirit find peace. At midnight on Christmas Eve the vicar celebrated Holy Communion alone, and in prayer invited the ghostly priest to join him. Together they took communion and it is claimed that after fulfilling his promise the priest never returned again.

If you want to visit the church and enjoy a wonderful glimpse of history I can well recommend a visit to the church in August. For one week the church is open to visitors, decked with flowers, full of old cuttings and photographs and other surprises. There is also an art exhibition, with pottery and needlework displayed. Lovely ladies cook wonderful food or you can be content with just a cup of coffee. What a delight.

SHADOWS OF THE PAST

++
The Five O'Clock Ghost
♦ ♦ ♦ ♦ ♦ ♦ ♦ ♦ ♦ ♦ ♦ ♦ ♦ ♦ ♦ ♦ ♦ ♦ ♦ ♦ ♦ ♦ ♦ ♦ ♦ ♦ ♦ ♦ ♦

On the island near Westgate Bridge now stands the
well-restored building known as the Westgate Galleria. For
years this historic building stood, lonely and derelict,
waiting for a decision on its future. The new roadways
leading to the Forest of Dean made its usefulness a problem
as it stood right in the middle of all the routes. Happily all
was resolved, it is now restored and if you give the building
the benefit of your time and consideration you will be well
rewarded.

It is not a museum and it is easy to forget just how many
uses the place had in times now forgotten. It was a haven
to the poor and needy for many generations, and stood just
inside the Gloucester boundary. Since the thirteenth
century the site has been used as a place of refuge and was
mentioned as far back as 1380 as 'a great house for the
poor'. It was named after St Bartholemew one of the twelve
apostles of Jesus Christ. In 1535 it was run by a Master with
five priests to administer to the inmates, and thirty-two
almspeople. Later, Queen Elizabeth I gave the place over
to the care of the Gloucester corporation. The home was
then enlarged. At the beginning of the eighteenth century
there was accommodation for twenty-four men and thirty
women.

The present structure was built at the end of the
eighteenth century in a Gothic style to replace the medieval
building. Over the years St Bartholemew's managed to

remain solvent by means of legacies left by rich people in the City of Gloucester. They wanted to ensure the poor were not forgotten. The position of the hospital ensured that poor and destitute people remained outside the city centre.

The hospital would have been very dull and austere by our standards. Inmates were strictly separated, which meant that impoverished married couples were unable to spend their remaining days together. The rules were severe, drab uniforms were provided, and the building would have been cold, damp and comfortless. Early rising was imposed and prayers were said before all meals and again at bedtime. The inmates were at least provided with a bed and felt fortunate to be sure of food to eat. There was no welfare state to turn to at that time, and anyone falling on hard times either through sickness or lack of work, or if a husband died leaving the widow and children penniless, the hospital or workhouse as it was called was the only answer.

Throughout the years the bishops of Gloucester made it their duty to keep a paternal eye on the administration, and would visit the poor.

The constant flooding was always a problem and the floor level was raised to improve the situation. It was not a comfortable place to be in. A working regime was imposed and inmates received a small wage in return for their labours. In 1830 this was raised to five shillings and six pence a week. Inmates were given their own small plot of land to till and grow vegetables. This would be a useful contribution to the home and a reminder of better times.

The present building now has a pleasant and ample restaurant. Sometimes in the evening the strains of a classic guitar can be heard playing to the diners. The food now served would have been a gourmet's delight to any of the former inmates. Gruel and a lump of bread is definitely not now on the menu. It was in the restaurant that we heard the story of strange hauntings claimed to be experienced by people now working there.

In the downstairs area when the staff are preparing to lock up and leave, the figure of a mischievous little girl dressed in what seems to be clothes from the Victorian era or earlier has sometimes been seen darting around the pillars. Five o'clock seems to be the time when this small child has been seen, darting about as if playing a game of Hide and Seek.

She is not the only figure claimed to have been seen. Colette who sometimes works in the restaurant said that an old man has appeared wandering around the top storey of the building by the stairs as if searching for his room. One minute he is there and the next he disappears.

Their presence is a ghostly reminder of hardships experienced in a time now past. The silent walls could surely tell many stories.

The Fish and Chip with Ghost Restaurant

Longsmith Street in Gloucester is in a very old part of the city not too far away from the Docks. The Black and White Restaurant sells quality fish meals to hungry tourists and the attractive little building has been there for five hundred years. Not as a fish and chip shop of course but previously as a private dwelling. The residents must have witnessed many changes in our history. Robert Raikes and his family would have passed the house frequently.

One fine Spring day in the beginning of April 1995 Eunice and James Phillips decided they would visit our city and take a look around. They travelled from Filton in Bristol together with their friends Eileen and Fred Hambley. After a successful morning they were all feeling hungry and decided to rest awhile in the Black and White Restaurant. They chose their table in the upstairs room then sat down and enjoyed the meal. At 1p.m. wishing to carry on exploring, the ladies said they would visit the toilet before setting off.

The friends went to use the toilet but saw a lady in grey

disappear into the room. They waited and waited for her to vacate the room. Now they were becoming anxious. They wondered what on earth could have happened to the lady, they even suggested that perhaps she had died in there. They called the waitress, Ann Little, who went upstairs to investigate but no one was there.

The senior citizens, convinced that they had seen someone go in the room and that no one had come out stated emphatically that they had not seen a ghost. The staff were unable to convince them otherwise, indeed they too have experienced ghostly goings on for many years in the place. Owner Mr Angelo Motto says that he has heard doors banging when the place has been empty and his wife Guilia says she too has seen someone running upstairs though she later found no one in the place.

They wondered if they should call in a priest to give the spirit peace, but when told this Colin Potts of Gloucestershire Tourism said a few friendly ghosts are sometimes good for business.

✦✦✦

The Old Regal Cinema

✦ ✦ ✦ ✦ ✦ ✦ ✦ ✦ ✦ ✦   ✦ ✦ ✦ ✦ ✦ ✦ ✦ ✦ ✦ ✦ ✦ ✦ ✦ ✦ ✦ ✦ ✦ ✦

Just nearby to King's Square once stood the Regal Cinema. This place was once the prime night spot of entertainment in Gloucester. It opened in a blaze of publicity in 1956. There was a grand gala performance on Monday 19 March. The film presented to the public was a Mario Zamni production in glorious technicolour called *Now and Forever*. It starred Janette Scott, Vernon Grey, Kay Walsh, and Jack Warner. Janette Scott made a personal appearance on the opening night, and crowds turned out to see her. The night was a sell out and the mayor of Gloucester, Alderman Langdon opened the celebratory show.

Courting couples soon made the cinema their favourite meeting place. Where else could young couples go for a cuddle? Few young people owned a car and the journey to

the cinema was made on foot by bus or bicycle. The cinema
made a big impact on the city. Television was not in every
home and videos were non existent. The cinema would be
in inky darkness once the performance had begun.
Usherettes holding a torch would show stumbling patrons
to their seats. At the end of the evening performance the
National Anthem would be played over the loudspeaker
and everyone would stand to attention. As the music
stopped there would be a mad scramble for the exit in order
to catch the last bus.

Now and Forever was hardly a prophetic title as
thirty-four years later in December 1990 the cinema closed.
A new Multiplex Cinema was opened in Peel Square
providing the necessary car spaces. *Mutant Turtles* were
the uninspiring stars of this event.

The Regal will never be forgotten, and it is interesting to
note that some of the staff of the Regal cinema spent all
their working life in the building. Dolly Green was once a
lifelong member of staff and said the cinema was something
that almost ran in her blood. Dolly and two other ladies said
they remembered when St Aldates's Church together with
a graveyard and a Church hall once stood on the site. Dolly
said she would play amongst the gravestones before Sunday
School began. The children had to be careful as it was a
Sunday and their best and only really decent clothes were
worn on this then special day.

David Browne said he too played around this area as a
small boy as building on the cinema started in 1939 and
stopped when the second world war began. Men and
materials were then needed for the war effort. Children in
Gloucester were quick to take advantage of this opportunity and the place soon became a popular play area. Little
footsteps would run in and out of the half built walls and
doorways. Staircases open to the sky proved a wonderful
challenge to the imagination of the children and many good
games were played.

Later the area became a storage place for the Ministry and
it was some time before the cinema was again started.

The Ghostly Regular

Dolly said the staff working at the cinema were aware of a cinema ghost. The projectionists claimed that sometimes during the showing of a film a ghostly figure would drift across the screen. Usherettes mentioned the strange feelings they experienced whilst working near the bottom right hand stalls. Cleaners did not like to work alone in the cinema and said they had spotted a dark figure sitting alone in the stalls. Staff bravely said they were not really frightened, but could not offer any explanation.

More recently in August 1995 I heard yet another spooky tale connected to the cinema. Mandy told me that her uncle Mr Syson worked in the cinema which on occasions was used as a theatre for stage performances. It was then, said Mandy, that things would begin to happen. Mr Syson would have a great deal of trouble with the broom which seemed to take on a life of its own. Apparently wishing to join the fun the broom would take off and dance across the stage. Mandy said that at the time it was claimed that the spirit was connected to the time when workmen were excavating the foundations for the cinema and discovered the remains of a coffin. Instead of being reconsecrated along with the other bodies from the graveyard the men just carried on digging and the remains were included in the foundations. The staff at that time wondered if that was why they had a dancing broom in the building. Who knows?

The Canon or Regal cinema together with what was once the beautiful church of St Aldates is now history. We will never be able to visit these places again.

Now after a great deal of controversy the empty building will become a public house again called The Regal. Building starts in October of this year.

Hugh Worsnip, the local journalist, made it known that if he ever came up on the lottery he would gladly spend the money on converting the cinema into a much needed theatre. Sadly it is too late for this to be possible. I wonder if the ghost will enjoy the pub as much as the cinema.

The Old Chemist Shop

Long time residents in Gloucester may remember the chemist shop Hamptons. It stood at the corner of St John's Lane on the Worcester Street side. Mr Reg Woolford the well known local historian told me at this time it was 47 Northgate Street. The premises of the chemist shop and Halfords the adjoining bicycle shop were later demolished and now belong to a building society.

In 1875 a chemist named Yeo Hughes used the premises and the shop remained as a chemist from that time right up until the 1960s.

Mr W.H. Hampton a respected gentleman took over the business in 1904 and served his customers right until 1965. Mr W.H. Hampton was described as a tall man with an upright carriage. He was a steward of Gloucester cathedral, and lived within walking distance of his business in a substantial house at 140 London Road.

In 1960 a young lady, then known as Bobby Winter, began work as an assistant in the chemist shop. One day Bobby had to go to the top of the building, where to her amazement she encountered the apparition of a young man dressed as if from another age. He appeared to her to be wearing what she could only describe as a ruff collar on his white shirt and black baggy trousers. He was not menacing, but he certainly startled the young girl. Not wishing to appear foolish the assistant carefully chose her words as she described the man to the other staff working there. They were amused and said that they too had seen the same spectre. Years later she can still describe the unusual occurrence to her daughters.

This incident took place right next to Halford's bicycle shop which is where a Mr Howells had a frightening experience when he was fourteen years old and a new employee of the cycle shop.

The unsuspecting lad went down the steps leading to the cellar where spare parts were stored and encountered on the stairs what he described as a grey solid mass about seven feet tall and three feet wide swirling about. Frightened and bewildered he ran up the stairs forgetting completely what he had been sent for and panted out his experience to the owner. The man was understanding but curious for when he went down the stairs the vision had vanished. All was then forgotten until some months later when the tramlines in the road outside were taken up, and, after a heavy storm, arriving to work in the morning, the owner discovered on descending the stairs the cellar was damp with rainwater and amongst the debris was a coffin which had come through the wall. At one time a graveyard was on the site of the shops. Perhaps the two incidents were connected.

The Spanish Ruff

Just one week after completing the previous account I was in Falmouth on holiday. It was there I came across a very useful article written by Gwen Methley a Falmouth historian. Gwen wrote about the Spanish ruff which was introduced to Britain in the sixteenth century. To achieve the round shape of the ruff, several layers of linen were placed one over the other, pleated like a fan and then starched. Starching became an art in itself. A pale blue-coloured rice was first used, this gave the ruff a bluish tinge. Then a rival pale yellow shade was invented by an English lady named Miss Turner.

Politics and religion it seems were even found in connection to linen and the blue dye was considered to be papist. Miss Turner's dye thus became popular with the protestants. Alas poor Miss Turner was unjustly accused of poisoning a Sir Thomas Overbury who died shortly after a visit from the lady. She was beheaded at the Tower of London. In defiance, Miss Turner went to the block wearing a dress with a pale yellow ruff. From that time it was understandably considered unlucky to wear a ruff of this colour and no elegant lady would wear one. All this happened in the years prior to 1643 the date of the Civil War of Gloucester.

Miss Winter who witnessed the ghost of the chemist shop was most emphatic that the young man she saw was wearing a ruff even though she knew nothing about the clothes worn at that time. We must conclude therefore that the ghost was a fashion conscious young man belonging to that era. Perhaps his death was in some way connected to the Civil War fought in Gloucester. Did he wear a papist blue ruff or a protestant yellow? We will never know.

Trouble at Work

Kim Martyn Goodey told us he was not much of a story teller, but he felt other people in Gloucester might like to hear of his experience.

In 1975 Kim was an apprentice carpenter in Gloucester. He was keen to learn his trade, and like most apprentices at that time if there was a boring routine job to do, it was the apprentice who drew the short straw. Above the workshop where he was learning his trade was another small business. A man working alone made his living by selling disco equipment. As one can imagine there was always music with a strong beat pounding out from above the room where Kim was working.

One evening about seven o'clock the man was working on a speaker. The job was going quite well and when he had finished he began to tidy up. He looked up and at the top of the stairs there stood the ghost of a woman watching him. He was so frightened by the apparition, he ran straight out of the room, down the stairs, and rushed to the nearest church. He told the vicar begging him to do something about it.

The vicar, seeing the genuine distress of the man, left his church and returned with him to his small one-room workshop. All was quiet and nothing strange happened. The vicar said prayers, and sprinkled holy water hoping to put the troubled spirit to rest. The experience was too much for the man who packed up his disco equipment and left hoping to relocate the workshop.

The empty room was then taken over by the carpenters. Now they had the two rooms, so Kim as apprentice was given the job of painting the vacant room. He put on his overalls, put the ten litre paint pot squarely on the strong table and set to work. In the corner of the room left behind by the previous tenant in haste stood a speaker grille. The room was long and narrow about twelve by forty feet across. Kim began to paint a door with emulsion paint. Suddenly he heard a rumble coming from the far end of the room, Kim looked up and to his amazement saw a grille fly across the room and hit him on the ankle as if someone had thrown it at him from a twenty foot distance. No one else was in the room. This mystified the young apprentice who ran downstairs to tell the boss who did not believe Kim at all. He put it down to the imagination of a teenage boy.

As it was just beginning to get dark the boss said, 'Leave the job and call it a day. Come back in the morning and you can get on with the painting.'

The next morning, not too troubled, Kim returned to the room. He got out the paint tin and placed it firmly on the table. He turned round and began to paint the door. There was a big crash behind him and the four legs of the strong solid table were flat on the floor out sideways. The ten litre paint tin was tipped over and the mess was horrendous. Kim said it was just as if someone had grabbed the legs sideways and pulled them hard. A task which would have confounded even the strongest of men. Paint was everywhere and again Kim ran down the stairs to tell his boss who thought he was just covering his tracks with a crazy excuse. The puzzled apprentice then got on with cleaning up the spilled paint.

From that day a series of mysterious occurrences took place. Almost every day for a week strange happenings would surprise the boy. Another morning Kim was sweeping up the sawdust after completing a job, when a large street map of London flew across the room from the bench where it had previously been resting. As he bent down, the map hit him sharply on the back. It had travelled from about twelve feet away.

Apart from the man in the disco workroom all the activity seemed to have been experienced by Kim. It seems that sometimes a poltergeist will manifest itself on young people who it seems are more susceptible to these things. Wishing to find out more about the place where they were working, and wondering about its previous history the men made enquiries and discovered that sometime in the past, possibly the eighteenth century there had been a fire and the house on the premises had been almost destroyed. A mother and two boys had perished. Kim concluded that perhaps the spirit of one of the boys had been his tormentor.

Later the firm moved to larger premises and nothing more seemed to happen. Kim who is now self-employed and is an accomplished carpenter with a good reputation, said that he will never forget the days when he was an apprentice troubled by mysterious events.

The story of Kim and the poltergeist were mentioned in *The Citizen* at that time together with a photograph of the haunted workshop.

◆◆◆
Cowboys and Indians in Gloucester
◆ ◆ ◆ ◆ ◆ ◆ ◆ ◆ ◆   ◆ ◆ ◆ ◆ ◆ ◆ ◆ ◆ ◆ ◆ ◆ ◆ ◆ ◆ ◆

This story is about the mysterious death of a man in Gloucester. He died there on 26 October 1676, after fighting a fierce battle with marauding Indians. The only difference is that it was in Gloucester, Virginia. There is more of a local connection to this story as the hero of our tale was Sir William Berkeley.

The Pilgrim Fathers first set foot in Virginia in 1606. They were very brave men indeed and worked hard to grow crops and make a living. They lived in a beautiful part of Virginia named Chesapeake Bay now famous for its quiet fishing holidays and wonderful crab restaurants. The settlements were beginning to do well but were threatened by the local Indians who followed their every move. One terrible night in 1622 it was reported that all but four were slaughtered out of five hundred. A terrible price to pay for their enterprise.

Now back for a short while to more recent times. In 1953 a precious book was presented to Gloucester library by Travis L. Berkeley Junior from the University of Virginia. It was a special copy of a book which was auctioned in 1913 for $5,100 dollars. The book was written by a Sir William Berkeley who was the first governor of Virginia. Sir William was a member of the famous aristocratic Berkeleys of Gloucester in England. Now there is a place named Berkeley in Virginia, after the same family. Berkeley is a vast plantation on the James River near Richmond. A place to put at the top of your visiting list when in that country. The wealth of the family came from the plantations which grew tobacco. It was there that the early settlers observed the very first Thanksgiving.

In 1642 Sir William Berkeley became the governor of Virginia. He was described as being of courteous bearing, lavish with his generosity which appealed to the loyal supporters of King Charles I of England. The Civil War was going on in England at that time, and some noblemen from Gloucester escaped to America to start a new life and save their necks at the same time.

When Sir William arrived there were twenty thousand colonists from the old country trying to make a living for themselves. In the book named *The Discourse and Views of Sir William Berkeley* it is mentioned that there were families there from Gloucestershire: the Percys, Berkeleys, Wests, Gages, Wyatts, Morrisons, Kemps, Chickaleighs, Moldsworths and many more. Perhaps your own families were there amongst them. The crops grown were flax, hemp, silk, wheat, barley, oats, rice, cotton and fruits. By far the best money spinner though was tobacco.

The Indians in their settlement were out for revenge. the war cry was heard, and the situation was desperate. Sir

William was furious that he had been disobeyed and said that 'If they had killed my Father and Mother and Friends, yet they came in peace they ought to have gone in peace'. He felt that as governor of Virginia his word should have been honoured. He refused to retaliate.

The planters were now being attacked on their homesteads by the Indians. They turned to Nathaniel Bacon to lead them. Nathaniel had his own plantation destroyed by the Indians and agreed to lead a rebellion. He was a skilled and capable commander. On one march he led his forces to drive the Pamunkey tribe into a swamp, and overpowered the Susquehannocks killing at least one hundred Indians and capturing others. Governor Berkeley was furious at the unauthorized attacks and sent his own troops to capture Nathaniel Bacon. For several weeks the battle raged, and eventually Nathaniel Bacon was caught and when he was brought before the governor he said that he repented. The governor then authorised his release and hoped the matter would be resolved.

Unlike Sir William Berkeley, Nathaniel was not a man of his word. He returned to capture Jamestown with an army of six hundred men, demanding a commission to fight the Indians. The governor was obliged under duress to give in, but later when Bacon set off to chase Indians, Governor Berkeley in his turn sent troops to bring back Nathaniel Bacon. The fighting became furious and was a vendetta between the two men which often did not involve the Indians at all.

Nathaniel recaptured Jamestown and burnt it to the ground. Berkeley retreated to the Eastern shore of Virginia and regrouped his troops for a final battle and confrontation which did not happen. Nathaniel Bacon who had suffered from malaria at Jamestown became seriously ill and died in Gloucester, Virginia on 26 October 1676. He was only twenty nine years old. The leader of the rebellion now dead, the rebellion fell apart and Governor Berkeley sent forces to capture what was left of Bacon's army. Some men were hanged on the gallows.

Sir William called tobacco a vicious, ruinous plant, bringing more money into the Crown than all the islands in America. It is strange that Sir William hated tobacco so much. Perhaps he was a non smoker. He may have had a hunch that it was bad for the health. The settlers however could not grow enough of it, and on it made their fortunes.

Tobacco was once grown around the Winchcombe area, but when it began to come in from Virginia, the local crops could not compete, and the fields were taken over for other uses.

The new governor was at first a popular man. He was a man of honour, who kept his word and principles whatever the price. He was soon to be severely tested by the Indians. In 1675 a great comet was seen in the sky. The settlers were often superstitious about things they could not understand and the word went round that this was a bad omen. Then came the flight of tens of thousands of pigeons, for days they blanketed out the sky and ate everything they could. The next Spring a plague of locusts arrived and ravaged the crops stripping every plant and tree in sight.

Next year a real disaster struck which affected all the pioneers and made them fight for their lives.

One quite Sunday an overseer named Robert Hen was found dying, nearby lay his dead Indian servant. As he gave his last breath, Hen gasped out the name Doegs! Which is the name of the tribe of Indians known for their fierce attacks. Sir William Berkeley was summoned and he wanted to solve the problem in an amicable way if it was possible.

There were others who cried out for revenge. They wanted to sort the matter out with an immediate confrontation. They had a leader for their cause, a man named Nathaniel Bacon. He too was wealthy and well educated. He was only twenty eight years old. Slim attractive and dark haired, with a fiery temper and a persuasive tongue, Nathaniel was a leader of men and a man of action. Sir William invited a party of six Indians to come in peace and discuss the situation. He gave his word they would not be harmed. This was not to be. The Indians approached the house of Sir William, an ambush under the leadership of Nathaniel Bacon set upon them and killed them.

The story soon travelled back to England in spite of the great distance. Sir William Berkeley was strongly criticized for the manner in which he handled the situation by both countries. He was sent home for an audience with the king, but died of a broken heart before he could give his own explanation. He felt he had been unjustly treated because he attempted to stay true to his word. What had begun as a great adventure to govern a new land for his king had ended as a tragedy of defeat. It was yet another example of a war in which there were only losers. Carnage and bloodshed was not a victory for anyone. It took many years for the new settlers to recover their previous prosperity.

Now comes the strange stories which followed this event.

For three months in 1676 about seventy of Nathaniel Bacon's followers lived in a large brick mansion just across the river from Jamestown, the scene of their battles. Since then the large house has been known as 'Bacon's Castle'. The house is very large with two oak panelled rooms on the first floor, two more on the second and an attic on the third. Nathaniel Bacon's followers it was said at the time were a rowdy group of men, who ransacked the place and caused havoc.

This ended when in 1676 at Christmas time a British ship named *Young Prince*, with Captain Robert Morris on board, landed with an order to capture the men. It is claimed the men slipped out of the house and escaped into the surrounding woods in darkness. Since that date there have been claims of many hauntings in 'Bacon's Castle'. A Mrs Charles Walter Warren who later lived there with her family said that in the twentieth century many strange occurrences have taken place. A velvet covered rocking chair is said to have rocked back and forward with no one in it. Footsteps have often been heard on the empty stairs.

One guest said she distinctly heard horrible moaning sounds coming from the attic. Outside the castle there have been claims from various people that they have seen a red fire ball floating around the house.

It seems that Gloucester in England and Gloucester in Virginia all have their problems.

INDEX

Numbers in italic represent illustrations